Forever Red

STEVE SMITH   *Confessions*
of a Cornhusker
Football Fan

University of Nebraska Press : Lincoln and London

Library of Congress Cataloging-in-Publication Data
Smith, Steve, 1970–
Forever red: confessions of a Cornhusker football fan /
Steve Smith.   p. cm.
ISBN-13: 978-0-8032-4310-1 (hardcover: alkaline paper)
ISBN-10: 0-8032-4310-3 (hardcover: alkaline paper)
1. University of Nebraska-Lincoln – Football.
2. Nebraska Cornhuskers (Football team) 3. Football
fans – Nebraska. I. Title
gv958.u53s65 2005   796.332'63'09782293–dc22
2005004656

For my family, and my friends,
and every Red Clad Loon
who ever took a dip in The Pond

CONTENTS

ACKNOWLEDGMENTS

One would think all this came flowing out of my obsessive fanboy brain and straight into print without any help. Not even close. I'd like to thank Catharine Huddle and Peter Salter for their keen eyes for detail; Julie Koch for her no-nonsense approach and critical eye; Kelly Steinauer, Casey Coleman, and Mary Jo Bratton for their timely help; Ted Kooser for his valuable time and equally valuable advice; Richard Piersol for knowing all the right people; Rob Taylor for *being* one of those people; and finally, Kathy Steinauer Smith for her love, support, enthusiasm, and patience as I paced the living room floor and talked through these ideas for what to her must have seemed like the millionth time. She can probably recite this book from memory, folks.

Saturday

You know that feeling? The one where it seems like it's a different day of the week than it really is? It usually occurs during the holidays or when your work schedule gets all screwed up. You go into the office Tuesday after Memorial Day, and you have to keep reminding yourself that it's not, in fact, Monday. Or worse, your boss has to remind you. And then you think, *Good grief, just how out of touch am I?* That's what I go through pretty much every day. In my mind it always seems to be Saturday.

It starts off innocently enough. Someone will come by my desk, perhaps, and mention what they watched on TV over the weekend. They'll say something about an episode of *The Sopranos* in which Robert Loggia made a cameo appearance. Before they're done my internal monologue is already going through the paces: *Robert Loggia's sure had some interesting parts over the years, hasn't he? Like when he played that growly assistant football coach in* Necessary Roughness. And that leads me to: *Hey, you know who else made an appearance in that movie? Roger Craig.* And the next thing you know, I'm at Memorial Stadium. Again. This time it's 1981, and Roger's dressed in red, jetting 94 yards down the Astroturf for a touchdown, with a pair of Florida State defenders helplessly flapping along in his wake. The school record for longest run from scrimmage that was, and it stood for twenty years, until Eric Crouch got 95 with that impossible run at Mizzou. And that gets me to consider: *Who'd win in a footrace between Crouch and Craig, if Craig were in his prime, of course? Hmmm . . .*

Eventually I come back to reality. Sometimes it's Friday, the Huskers are in town tomorrow, and the whole state is alive with anticipation. And sometimes it's just an ordinary Wednesday in July, fall camp is still a month away, and the whole state is dying of boredom. So I check the clock at HuskerPedia.com, which counts down the days, hours, minutes, and seconds until the season's first kickoff. It's not moving fast enough.

About then, a tiny spark of self-awareness tells me that this is just not how well-adjusted adults act. Well, I'm not a well-adjusted adult.

I'm a Nebraska fan. This is what we do. We obsess about the Huskers – some of us more than others, and I'm among the "some of us" not the "others."

Nebraska fans are legendary for their devotion. You hear about guys all the time who boast of attending 357 consecutive home games, usually wearing the same red windbreaker and lapel-pin-covered trucker hat. These are men who spend their free time in basement "war rooms" festooned in Cornhusker paraphernalia. Their dogs are named Frazier, Osborne, or Rozier, and their Fords have bumper stickers proclaiming Memorial Stadium the state's third-largest city. They go to Misty's on Friday nights in the fall, tailgate with their wives the next day, and frown on scheduling weddings anytime between September and January. And when the subject of the Memorial Stadium home game sellout streak comes up, they assume the same gushy expression they had the day their children were born. These are tried-and-true fans to be sure.

And then you've got people like me. I don't need a media guide to come up with top-of-the-head gimmes like the number of yards we gained rushing without being stopped for a loss against New Mexico State in '82 (677) or which wideout holds the record for most touchdown catches in the Spring Game (Riley Washington with three) or why Cory Ross wore No. 22 his first two years before switching to No. 4 as a junior (he wore No. 4 through high school, but the number was occupied by Judd Davies during Ross's freshman and sophomore years at Nebraska, so those years he put on No. 22, or two plus two). I also can't resist the urge to inject the Big Red into everyday conversations. Doesn't matter what the topic is – politics, pop culture, the economy – I can always find a way to refer to Nebraska football and give my friends an opportunity to look at me with bewildered amazement and/or pity. Last, I can say sincerely that of all of Martin Scorsese's films I like *Casino* best – and not because of Joe Pesci's fake Chicago accent, Robert DeNiro's malleable mug, or even Sharon Stone's comely derriere. I like it because in the final eight seconds of this three-hour picture, there's a lovely, bittersweet closing scene in which the tragic hero, sitting in his living room on a fall afternoon, poignantly accepts his lot in life, and there, off in the background and out of focus, Nebraska is playing on his TV. This is the kind of thing that separates good cinema from great cinema.

I consider myself lucky that my obsession is dressed in scarlet and cream. And I'm fortunate that through the years that fixation has withstood occasional bouts of apathy, grief, and downright disgust. It's carried on through advancing age, evolving interests, expanding worldviews, and frequent zip code changes. Seems like no matter where I am or what I'm doing, a Saturday at Memorial Stadium is always just a few daydreams away.

So, welcome to my world. Welcome to a place where it's always Saturday.

Rosalie

The Beginning

So there we were, rumbling south down Highway 77 in our Chevy Impala on our way to a football game, when my dad became my hero and the Nebraska Cornhuskers my team for life.

It happened, oddly enough, over the CB radio, the best in-car entertainment in those pre–Game Boy days. The drive to Lincoln from Rosalie, our tiny town of two hundred in the northeast corner of the state, wasn't exactly jam-packed with excitement. There was the traditional pit stop at the Fremont Dairy Queen to look forward to or maybe even an interlude at the corner café in Wahoo. Thankfully, until my oldest sister had decided she was going to the university after high school, Lincoln wasn't a trip I had to endure very often. In the decades that followed – through hundreds of Big Red victories, a couple dozen losses, and thousands of dollars spent on jerseys, sweatshirts, commemorative videos, and season tickets – Lincoln would become the epicenter for nearly every emotion I had, but before 1980 it was just a really long way away. Until then the longest trip I had taken was to Sioux City, some forty miles away, to get school clothes at JCPenney. Lincoln was at least twice as far as that – far enough that we'd have to stop for gas on the way.

My sister hadn't come home to Rosalie for a visit since she left for school in mid-August. My father managed the service station along Highway 77, three miles east of town, and he worked six days a week, fifty-one weeks a year, but he figured if he was ever going to see his oldest daughter again, he was going to have to take a Saturday off, clean the grease from under his fingernails, and drive down to see her. September 20 was to be the first of what presumably would be many trips south over the next four years.

The first time, though, was special; there was something more – a bonus. Two weeks earlier Dad announced at the dinner table that he had pulled a few strings and gotten four tickets to the upcoming Nebraska-Iowa game. This was a big damn deal. People from really small towns typically did not go to Husker games. Such indulgences were reserved for businessmen in Pender, the county seat, or for rich

3

farmers. We finished the meal feeling like we had come upon a winning $84 million lottery ticket.

My dad admonished me and my middle sister, who was fourteen, against boasting openly about going – mainly because he was protective of his property, to the point of being paranoid, and didn't want anyone else to know we'd be away for an entire day. But also the crowd at Smith's Standard Station would see going to Lincoln to a game as some kind of elitist, upper-crust activity. This would not mesh well with my dad's constant labor to avoid any appearance of being different from anyone else in Rosalie. That wasn't hard because we weren't, really. Like all of our neighbors, our family drove an American car, ate red meat, watched CBS, and had a blue-collar patriarch under our roof who drank Budweiser and voted a straight Republican ticket. We viewed the lifestyles of people in Lincoln and Omaha much the way people in Lincoln or Omaha probably viewed the lifestyles of people in Amsterdam or Barcelona – distant, foreign, and basically irrelevant, except maybe as a source of hypothetical interest or curiosity. Apparently that was changing, thanks to my oldest sister. When she moved to Lincoln to broaden her horizons, she forced us to broaden ours too.

This would be my first game, but the Huskers were not exactly an unknown quantity. Simply because I had been living and breathing for nine consecutive years within Nebraska's borders, I knew what the Cornhuskers were: pretty damn good, that's what. Also, I knew that their coach was the red-haired Tom Osborne and that the radio announcer yelled hilarities into his microphone when things went particularly well. The school song was "There Is No Place Like Nebraska"; I knew that one because my dad's friend had a car horn that played the tune. People wore red-and-white shirts and caps quite a bit and seemed to talk a lot about the team, even in the summer months when the Cornhuskers weren't playing. It would be some time until I fully understood the important territory the team occupied in Nebraskans' collective consciousness, but I was old enough to feel Husker football's formidable presence and grasped the general concept that it was significant and special, that it was *our thing*.

As we bounced southward down the highway that Saturday morning, channel 16 on the CB picked up two Hawkeye fans, presumably also on the way to Lincoln. It was clear they liked the Hawks' chances. After all, they argued, the year before the mighty Huskers had to rely on a last-second field goal to steal a road victory. And though it was early in the season, conventional wisdom said the Hawkeyes were a better team this year. The Cornhuskers were about to be ambushed.

"Oh, baby, Big Red's gonna get beat today," one of them cackled. "Don't know what's going to hit 'em!"

Until that point my father was content to just listen in and let the poor, misguided boobs have their fun. But now they had crossed a line. He seized the mike. "Big Red get beat? Bull*shit*," Dad said.

What followed was a colorful radio conversation that included but was not limited to Nebraska's powerful running attack, Iowa's knock-off-Pittsburgh-Steelers uniforms, the Cornhuskers' Doberman-like defense, Iowa's wholly overrated leading rusher, and the fact that the closeness of last year's game was an accident precipitated by unforced Nebraska turnovers. I don't remember exactly how the tête-à-tête ended, except that near the end my father boldly predicted that Iowa would be lucky to score, that the game would be basically over by halftime, and that the Husker backups would be mercifully dispatched to mop up for a sizeable chunk of the second half.

And off it went – the first tiny flame of my fandom was sparked. I would love to say that it actually happened during a sepia-toned afternoon at the old ballpark while Dad and I shared a stadium dog and then mix in a few Springsteen lyrics about him tousling my hair, setting me on his lap, and telling me to take a good look around. But instead it came in the backseat of the Impala, my fourteen-year-old sister whining about my leg being on her side of the car as my dad dropped the Hammer of Thor on a couple of uppity Iowans. We still had more than an hour to go to get to Lincoln, but I'd already experienced one of the day's highlights. Plus, my anxiety over the game, which I had felt building in the pit of my stomach all morning, suddenly subsided. My father, the chief authority and influence in my life, pronounced gallantly that the Cornhuskers were going to win, and win big. I could kick back and relax.

It didn't take long that afternoon for Nebraska to get into the end zone and to start its unavoidable beatdown of the early season opponent. In my mind's eye, I can see that first touchdown clearly: Jeff Quinn, the quarterback from Ord, takes the snap, turns and shovels a quick pitch out to Jarvis Redwine, the swivel-hipped I-back with a quarterback's number; No. 12 gathers in the ball near the west sideline, slips past a defender, makes a clever cutback move about 5 yards past the line of scrimmage, and then gallops half the length of the field into the end zone – the south end zone, where we were sitting, sixty-five rows up. It was the first big run by a Cornhusker I-back I'd experienced, and over the years it would serve as my mental blueprint for all great Nebraska backs taking that same pitch and running to daylight and glory.

What I remember most about that first trip to Memorial Stadium, however, isn't touchdowns and tackles. It is everything else. The game was played in that jungle-style kind of heat that can make people just burst into flames. On the way into the stadium Dad bought me a balloon to release upon NU's first touchdown, and it damn near melted in the sun before I could let it fly, barely two minutes in. The band cranked out "Hail Varsity," a second, more regal school song to go along with the one I already knew. The big orange scoreboard flashed messages for businesses like First Federal Lincoln and the Monsanto Company. I had the odd sense that everyone but us had been here before, that everyone else here was from much bigger towns than we were, and that they knew the whole drill a lot better. They recognized when it was time to do the "Go Big Red (clap)! Go Big Red (clap)!" cheer, and when they did it was in perfect unison, almost as if it were choreographed. Suddenly I felt very small.

Perhaps most, it was the bigness of it all that transfixed me – from the booming, omnipresent PA announcer to the sheer massiveness of the press box to that low, earthy rumble that erupted into a wall of noise when Quinn or Redwine or Anthony Steels or Derrie Nelson or any other red-jerseyed wildman made a big play, giving everyone a reason to leap from their seats, release guttural noises, and punch the air. By halftime it was 35-0 on the way to 57-0, and my father's pregame pronouncement to the insolent Iowans came back: *They'll be lucky to score; the game'll be over by halftime* . . . It had gone just as he had said it would. When it was all over, my imagination had been suitably captured – in the free moments of the days, weeks, and months that followed, that glorious, bright-red spectacle was just about the only thing I would, or could, think about.

So that's how it got started. No drawn-out application process, no lengthy deliberation, just some smack-talking from my father, overpriced parking by the Fourteenth Street railroad tracks, and one long, superlative burst of scarlet. Like the hapless Hawkeyes, I was completely inundated with red that day.

I suppose that if it had just been an uneventful ride down to the game and Dad hadn't gotten into it with those Hawkeyes, I still would've walked away a fan, so overpowering was that first encounter with the Big Red. Two weeks later I listened as Lyell Bremser mournfully described how Quinn's fumble at the Florida State 3-yard line ended Tom Osborne's shot at an undefeated year, and it hurt – but it didn't matter. We were sitting in the parking lot of the Southern Hills Mall in Sioux City, Mom had just bought me a new red T-shirt, and I was in this for the long haul.

High Octane

NEBRASKA 48, OKLAHOMA STATE 7 – OCTOBER 18, 1980

At a very early age, usually about the time walking and talking are under control, every child in a Devaney-fearing Nebraska home is introduced to Football Saturday. This is, one quickly learns, a holy day when everyone douses himself in red clothing – some of it faded, some of it too small for expanded midsections, but red nonetheless. Meantime, the American flags on big white houses in places like Fremont and Wayne and West Point are supplanted by red ones with big block *N*s. And on Football Saturdays, you can go into any building, anywhere in the state and hear the Nebraska game on the radio.

In 1980 radio was a lifeline for Nebraskans on Football Saturday. They had four stations to choose from – it was just a few years before Bob Devaney, as the athletic director in pursuit of as many Benjamins as possible, narrowed the Cornhusker broadcasting field to one originating station in an exclusive deal – KFOR or KLIN out of Lincoln, or wow or KFAB out of Omaha. But honestly, it didn't matter to my brood. We were a one-station family. On fall Saturdays our dials were dutifully cemented at 1110 AM, the residence of one Lyell Bremser.

By that drizzly mid-October day, Lyell was going on his forty-first year of woofing out his unique brand of play-by-play. For more than four decades, he'd repeatedly beckoned the men, women, and children to listen in. It was Bremser's turns of phrase that were repeated to roars of laughter at Sunday school the next morning.

The day Nebraska hosted 0-4 Oklahoma State, I went to work with my dad because my mom had to clerk at the Rosalie Post Office in the morning. As he often did on Saturdays, Dad took the fuel tank-wagon out for a few deliveries. After five days of pounding on tires and changing farmers' oil, it was nice to have some time away from the station. Further, the tankwagon had a damn good AM radio.

The first stop was a farm west of Rosalie. On a normal day there would have been plenty of things for a fourth grader to talk about with his dad: school, hunting, cars, the genius that was Kenny Rogers, and so on. But today Bremser's voice was the only one getting a workout. And in the time it took us to drive the seven miles to the first delivery, Lyell had informed us that Nebraska had, as expected, bolted into the lead over the sad-sack Cowboys. The first score was courtesy of a Jeff Quinn pass to tight end Jeff Finn.

Minutes later Bremser described one of the day's most memorable plays: Quinn drops back to pass and throws toward wingback Anthony "Slick" Steels near the goal line. But, oops, Oklahoma State's Greg Hill gets in the way at the 15 and tips the pigskin up into the air. The ball flutters toward Steels, No. 33, at the 5, but he can't gather it in, so he gives the football an underhand tap and sends it fluttering into the air again. By the time Slick reaches the 1, the ball settles in his hands for good, and he skips into the end zone, untouched, for 6 points. Touchdown, Nebraska – just like they drew it up.

As we headed north toward the next delivery, Nebraska's fortunes took a bit of a dip. The Huskers had installed an option offense, and when they weren't rumbling, they were fumbling. On successive drives NU fumbled twice then had a punt blocked. Nebraska got it together in time to stick in a late second-quarter touchdown to go up 21-0, and while that made me feel a bit better, apparently I was the only one. There was a tone in Lyell's voice that reflected what everyone else in the Cornhusker State was thinking: *This thing's a lot closer than it's supposed to be, dadgummit.*

Things got worse before they got better. The second half had started just as Dad was stopping the tankwagon for the fifth delivery, and sure enough, fullback Andra Franklin coughed the ball up again. When the Cowboys scored to pull within 21-7, Dad grunted, then climbed out of the cab and onto the top of the tankwagon, leaving me with Lyell.

The Cornhuskers, apparently awakened by the sight of the visiting Cowboys actually putting points on the scoreboard, pulled off the kid gloves. What followed was an onslaught that overwhelmed and crushed the pitiful Pokes. Craig Johnson with the ball – Touchdown! Roger Craig on the carry – Touchdown! Johnson takes the handoff again – Touchdown!

After each score, I climbed out of the cab and yelled gleeful updates to my father. He'd yell back, making sure he had heard me right: "Twenty-eight seven? Thirty-five seven? *Forty-two* seven?" By the time the last stop's tank was full, that little OSU insurrection had been quashed right quick, order had been restored, and Jimmy Johnson's pretenders were fading from the almighty Big Red's rearview mirror.

I'd eventually come to learn that this was no big deal, not really. There was one of these Husker scoring flurries every time our boys played a sorry-ass Big 8 team. We knew it was coming, they knew it was coming, the officials knew it was coming, Tom Osborne's pastor's Chihuahua knew it was coming. It was only a matter of time – at some point the outmanned opponent's jig would be up and the thrashing would be on.

But Lyell Bremser, true to form, made it sound like he was the most shocked son of a gun in the state when the anvil finally fell, and fell hard, on the Okies. And so I was surprised by the outburst too. That was the beauty of radio. It wasn't just part of the game, it *was* the game. The announcer's word was law – robbed of your sight, you channeled his surprise, his anxiety, his excitement, and his indignation at a lousy call. And if Lyell Legend was surprised by a 21-point blitzkrieg, then I was too.

In a decade's time, the College Football Association would wither to dust and so would its rules restricting the number of times a school could be shown on TV each autumn. The major conferences, along with independent Notre Dame, would jockey for multimillion-dollar TV deals, meaning Nebraska's games against four-touchdown mutts like Troy State would get at least regional coverage and an 11 a.m. kickoff. But in 1980 the red-and-white world built by Lyell Bremser's nasal staccato was all we had, and in that reality, the Cornhuskers were giants that walked the earth.

Today, only the dinkiest of Nebraska towns are without cable TV. And there, local taverns will pony up for a satellite dish so they can host community-wide watch parties. So for the big majority of Nebraskans, there's no mystery in following the Cornhuskers, and certainly no room for artistic interpretation. Football Saturday has become a high-definition spectacle – football for consumption, no imagination required. I'll take it, of course, since we obsessive fans will take as much of our object of obsession as we can get. But while TV is more, it's not necessarily better.

Look no further than TV announcers. They're resigned to merely keeping the pictures on the screen company because they know their words can't do them justice. And TV's made us lazier as fans: Each week, live on our thirty-seven-inch flatscreens, the players – their mannerisms, their strengths, and more important, their flaws – are served up to us on a silver platter. And a fat lot of good it does us. TV's given us access to vast amounts of information about the game, but we aren't more knowledgeable.

It would have been a fishes-and-loaves-style miracle for the Oklahoma State game to have been on TV that day, given the restrictions at the time. If I'd been able to actually watch Anthony Steels grab that wacky touchdown pass after batting it around in the air as he ran, I might have decided it was just the result of some dumb luck. But to hear Bremser tell it, Slick knew exactly what he was doing; he was just waltzing into the end zone with some style, and the masses listening around the state were none the wiser. In Lyell's world, Nebraska was just *that much better* than everyone else.

I once heard someone say that any resemblance between Lyell Bremser's account of the game and the actual happenings on the field was purely coincidental. This was, for many a Nebraska fan, probably a good thing.

Busted

OKLAHOMA 21, NEBRASKA 17 - NOVEMBER 22, 1980

Let's just get this out there: It's pretty easy to be a follower of the Nebraska Cornhuskers. If you hear someone on sports talk radio claiming to be a "long-suffering Husker fan," you have every right to call him an idiot. The guy is probably just a pissed-off-at-the-world septuagenarian for whom a ten-win season is a legitimate reason to pout until March, or else he's been watching the Husker basketball team by mistake. In general, supporting Nebraska's football team is a breeze. The Huskers almost always win; over the past four decades, Nebraska has posted a must-be-a-misprint winning rate of upward of 80 percent, many of those wins blowouts. So you're not risking a lot by donning red on Saturdays to follow a team that could basically win nine games by running the I-back off-tackle every play. The return on your emotional investment is pretty high.

Most Saturdays during my childhood, Nebraska didn't so much play football as engage in ritual sacrifices. In 1980 alone the Huskers beat Utah 55-9, Iowa 57-0, Kansas 54-0, Oklahoma State 48-7, Colorado 45-7, Kansas State 55-8, and Iowa State 35-0. That win over the Iowa State Cyclones was a veritable nail-biter. Supporters of almost any other school would be giddy with such swollen results, but not Nebraskans. We knew that most everyone on NU's schedule wasn't really in our class, so nine touchdowns on offense and a shutout by the defense is what was expected. September and October – and much of November, come to think of it – were reserved for punishing the puny humans for having the gall to even entertain the notion they were in Nebraska's league.

Through this, it became easier and easier to believe our players were cut not only from a superior athletic cloth but from a superior academic, moral, and spiritual one as well. After all, the team was a reflection of us, the God-fearing, rules-abiding citizens of the Plains. We're good people, so they're good people, as the understanding goes: The white helmet and the red jersey embody deeply felt traditions that are expressed on the football field, because that team comes from us and from our history. On Saturday afternoons, the Cornhuskers are more than a pack of muscle-bound college kids running around in colorful padding. They're emblematic of us, of our way of life, and through their wins they strike mighty blows in our perpetual fight to show the rest of the country how good we are.

In the 1980s there was always one big end-of-the-year opportunity for affirmation of our superiority, and it always came against the University of Oklahoma. Sure, going into places like Ames, Iowa, and Manhattan, Kansas, and decimating their impotent home-standing squads was a nice distraction on a Saturday, but it was hard to get much psychic comfort when the biggest question going in wasn't whether Nebraska would win but rather by how much. Oklahoma, they were another story altogether. They were another superpower, a lot like us.

But they were a lot different too. For one, there was always an outlaw element to the Sooners, which stood in stark contrast to our wholesome Huskers. In Tom Osborne, Nebraska had a soft-spoken coach who was a milk-drinking preacher's grandson. In Barry Switzer, Oklahoma had a slick-talking boss who was the offspring of bootleggers. Nebraska's starting lineup was made up of fresh-faced fourth-year juniors and fifth-year seniors who had waited their turn and paid their dues; Oklahoma's was peppered with flashy freshmen and slapdash sophomores. Nebraska's style of play was staid and cerebral; Oklahoma's, with its speedy wishbone, was a high-wire act unparalleled in terms of entertainment value. Oklahoma's play often was called "basketball on grass," and that seemed to make sense. I used to think basketball players were cool because they played their games at night, and like all people who came out at night, they had a bit of hoodlum in them. Oklahoma had sex appeal. Nebraska, in a word, didn't.

The Huskers came into the game 9-1 and ranked fourth. Oklahoma, after starting the season 3-2 and needing a dramatic rally to nip eternally wretched Kansas State in Manhattan, had climbed to No. 9. Because the rest of the Big 8 Conference had difficulty tying their shoes on fall Saturdays, the winner of this end-of-the-world showdown in Lincoln would be the league champ and represent the conference at the Orange Bowl in Miami. Nebraska was an odds-on favorite; with the insertion of an option package into its already explosive offense, the Big Red had become a point-scoring juggernaut in 1980. The defense was also correctly rock-ribbed, giving up fewer than 10 points a game and among the nation's leaders in every statistical category. And the game was at home. Conventional wisdom bellowed Nebraska was going to dispatch OU, then march off to Miami and avenge its only loss of the season in a rematch with Florida State.

Despite all of the pregame puffery, the mood around my family's dinner table was one of caution. Since I'd heard his bold prediction over the CB radio in September, I'd turned to my all-knowing father each Friday night for a preview of the next day's events. Nearly every week I'd seek some affirmation from Dad, who would dutifully predict a Cornhusker blowout, laced with a few appropriately vague references – "I think Redwine will have a good number of yards rushing," "The defense'll get a couple turnovers tomorrow" – and the next day, the Cornhuskers would deliver on his promises. But when I asked him for his thoughts the Friday before the Oklahoma game, he gave a quick response: "I don't *know*, Bud." And that's when I realized that Dad, faced with having to make a real prediction, was scared. A season's worth of mental fortification, built on hog-stompings over Iowa State and K-State, wilted away with the prospect that my old man was doubting the boys.

So I watched the game with my mom. Well, that is to say I watched the game, and my mom checked in every five minutes or so while she worked off her nervous energy by washing dishes, dusting the furniture, defrosting the refrigerator, changing the oil in the Impala, building on a new two-story wing to our house, and so on. And contrary to the ingrained statewide inferiority complex that convinced us the worst possible thing was about to happen, the game actually started well for the Huskers. Six minutes in, the Big Red was backed up to its own 11 when Jeff Quinn slid down the right side of the line. He flipped the ball to "Marvelous" Jarvis Redwine. No. 12 slipped past a Sooner lineman in the backfield, got a key block from fullback Andra Franklin, shrugged off a defensive back at the corner, and proceeded to outrun the entire Oklahoma defense. At the OU 20, he looked back and pointed his left index finger at a flailing Sooner defender, taunting him. For a moment, I wondered if the TV's color was off. Such snide gestures were reserved for Oklahoma's running backs, not ours. But as Jarvis crossed the goal line, I forgot my brief moment of embarrassment. Touchdown – it was almost too easy. Sweet heavens, the next thing I knew NU had tacked on a field goal. The bus was warming up for Miami.

But then the game tightened up, as nearly all Nebraska-Oklahoma games do. After getting stuffed by the Blackshirts for much of the first half, OU suddenly pulled two scores out of its hat and waltzed into the locker room up 14-10. Then the game settled into a maddening defensive tone – Nebraska was keeping the 'Bone in check, but the offense, after Jarvis made it seem so damn *effortless* at the outset, became about as potent as a mixed drink in a strip joint. It seemed like the Huskers ran the fullback dive about four hundred times in the third quarter alone, with little success.

It was looking like curtains. But then, with the clock winding down, the Huskers finally caught a break. Oklahoma's punter shanked one off the side of his foot, the ball dribbling out of bounds at the Sooner 17. The Cornhuskers banged it in four plays later on a Quinn sneak, and suddenly it was 17-14 with just over three minutes to play.

Sensing victory, Mom stopped scrubbing the kitchen ceiling and joined me in the living room. She turned the volume up, stood back with her hands on her bony hips, and made a comment about how happy she was for the team. For the first time all day, I lowered my shoulders and allowed myself to exhale. And as if on cue, Oklahoma proceeded to race down the field, chewing up huge chunks of real estate with desperate Cornhuskers flailing aimlessly behind, and scored the winning touchdown with less than a minute to play. Buster Rhymes – a freshman, of course – did the honors. Ballgame, Oklahoma.

I spent the evening in my room, deconstructing the day's events. I couldn't figure out what had happened, much less why. I had been led to believe Nebraska had the better team, both in and out of uniform. And I had been led to believe the good guys always won, or at least had a damn good chance when playing at home as a 5-point favorite.

The next morning, looking over the Omaha paper's account of the game, I came to realize that even as a fan of a team that wins as many games as easily as Nebraska does, you're still immensely vulnerable. It's not the same vulnerability that fans of traditional doormats like, say, Kansas experience on a week-in, week-out basis, but it's real just the same. To climb so far that you can nearly reach the summit, to be so damn close to the promised land that you can almost taste it and then in a flash just have it disappear – this was the cruel fate of a Nebraska fan.

My dad liked to say that those impossible Oklahoma wins, and the epic Nebraska crash-and-burns that went with them, were good for us. They reminded us that life wasn't fair and that more often than not, style could kick substance's ass. He also liked to say that there was always next year.

The Scapegoat and the Savior

NEBRASKA 17, AUBURN 3 – OCTOBER 3, 1981

A wise man once said that a good scapegoat is almost as good as a solution. I have no idea who that wise man was, but in 1981 it may as well have been Mark Mauer.

Mauer was a tall, good-looking guy who, according to KMTV 3

14

sports anchor Terry Yeager, could sing and play the guitar. He also was a pretty solid student by all accounts. And he happened to be under center during the first game of the year, when the Big Red left for Iowa City as three-touchdown favorites and came home 3-point losers.

Oh, the score was only 10-7 (and dammit, if Phil Bates could've just lifted his feet a little more on that fourth-quarter run, he probably would have broke it for the winning touchdown), but the final tally might as well have been 100-0, so humiliating was the defeat. I only heard it on the radio, but it was clear the team was bewildered by the Hawks. And worst of all, this loss was to a program that at the time had endured twenty straight losing seasons.

Getting bushwhacked by Iowa in early September wasn't exactly in the same category as bowing to Oklahoma in late November and having to settle for the Sun Bowl. No, this was one of those full-blown, gee-I-hope-no-one's-waiting-for-us-at-the-airport-so-we-can-get-home-under-cover-of-night catastrophes. The aftershocks rolled across every inch of the state and reshuffled our unwritten pecking order – as self-deprecating as we Nebraskans could be, we always had Iowa to look down our noses at, in a football sense, anyway. Now that was gone too.

Someone had to pay for this indignation. And the Husker-following public, including the bib-overalled cabal that huddled around the Smith's Standard Station radio on Saturdays, determined that someone to be Mark Mauer. Though he was a senior, Mauer was a first-time starter and had seen only limited playing time until his start in Iowa City. Until then, his resume chiefly consisted of pitching the ball to second- and third-string tailbacks after NU was safely ahead of Lugnut State by seven touchdowns. But against Iowa, Mauer personified the Huskers' incompetence, from throwing a first-quarter interception to, unforgivably, fumbling away a center exchange in the fourth quarter, which pretty much clinched the Hawkeye upset.

Of course, Mauer wasn't the only one who played poorly. Roger Craig was apparently so excited to be playing in front of his home-state fans that he dropped the ball every other time he carried it. The offensive line was leaking like a sieve. Iowa held onto the football for what must have been the entire third quarter by ramming the ball straight at our downy chick–like defensive interior. And, at the risk of sounding like Arthur Fonzarelli trying to say he's sorry, I'll attempt to type these words without retching – *Iowa had a damn good team that year.* The Hawks won eight games, got a piece of the Big 10 title, and represented their conference at the Rose Bowl. As the fall rolled on, it turned out the Hawkeyes could play some ball. Their win wasn't a fluke.

Didn't matter. As far as our household – and every other household across an anxious state sweltering in the early September heat – was concerned, this whole mess was brought on by one guy's incompetence. Where the hell did they get this Mauer guy, anyway? By the time I walked to school Monday morning, Mauer's name had been cursed approximately 3.7 million times. And that was just at *our* house.

The quarterback is and always will be the easiest player to blame for our woes. For as knowledgeable as we like to think we are about the sport, the average Nebraskan doesn't know the difference between the single wing and a buffalo wing. When the game is on TV, we're not studying the intricacies of line play or grading the fullback on his blocking. Our eyes just follow the quarterback, and we form all of our opinions from there. The loss to Iowa wasn't even televised, but in the week that followed, the airwaves and letters to the editor were full of suggestions on what to do with Mauer: Make him run wind sprints. Bench him. Revoke his scholarship. Drive him out to a country road outside Deshler and kick him out of the car. Nothing seemed too ruthless.

Such meanspirited vitriol exists everywhere. But in Nebraska, where fans expect constant victory, it takes on a distinctive slant. We're quick to point fingers, but we first look for someone on our own team at whom to point them. The usual suspects – the incompetent officials, the disruptive weather, the incessant crowd noise, even the dirty bastards on the other side of the ball who beat us – are spared our wrath upon initial review. In our ongoing, heroic efforts to find out exactly what went wrong, our first impulse is to look to our own sideline, because we know, deep down, that the Cornhuskers are so good that the only responsible party for a Nebraska loss is, well, Nebraska. No one else, including the other team, really has a say in the game's outcome. If it's not our lousy quarterback, then it's the coach's erratic play calling. If it's not that, then it's not having the best players on the field at the same time. If the Huskers somehow get that right and are still outmatched by the other team, well, then our coaches didn't do a good enough job recruiting, and that's why we lost.

The more self-aware fans realize the ridiculousness of this self-reproach. But some still try to justify it: When the Huskers lose to a 21-point underdog, to deny you don't want to punch the quarterback's lungs out is to deny your own humanity. Partaking in a good bit of name-calling and finger-pointing merely shows you care passionately about the team, its success, and its long-term well-being. It shows that you're loyal. It shows that you're a True Fan.

For me it came down to a simple matter of helplessness. I'd learned after the previous year's heartbreaker to Oklahoma that if you're born in Nebraska, your allegiance to the Cornhuskers is not something about which you have a choice. It's something you're stuck with. A number of times over the last quarter century – usually the Sunday after a rare but gut-wrenching loss – my left brain has filed a stack of cease-and-desist orders against my right brain in hopes of voiding my emotional contract with the team once and for all, only to find it unbreakable. Sitting in the stands, or in front of the TV or the radio, as the team struggles and knowing you can't just walk away but that there's also nothing you can do can just about kill a guy. At least when you point fingers and assign blame, you're doing something.

So when Tom Osborne announced midweek that he was making a change at quarterback, a collective cheer that could have been measured on the Richter scale filled the air. And a few days later, behind fleet-footed but noodle-armed Nate Mason, Nebraska put the wood to Florida State. For one sunny Saturday, order had been restored. Unfortunately, it lasted only until grim word arrived that Mason had blown out his ankle in the game and was gone for the year. The No. 3 Penn State Nittany Lions were coming to town in six days, and as far as our quarterback situation went, we'd just made a bad spin in the Game of Life – TORNADO BLOWS YOU BACK TO START. Predictably, Mauer presided over a moribund 30-24 home loss to Penn State, a game that sounded closer than it really was. The defeat caused the Cornhuskers to do the unthinkable – they dropped out of the AP Top 20 for the first time since Grant took Richmond. To this day, it's the only time I can actually remember Nebraska entering October with a losing record.

Things were starting to come unraveled. Though they tried to hide it by looking at their boots and scuffing the floor with them as they stood near the grease pit, the regulars at Smith's Standard Station had a genuine sense of panic setting in. One of them, a farmer who lived along Highway 77 and had a red barn with "Go Big Red" painted on it, was considering repainting it to say, "Big Red's Dead." He was serious. To compound matters, Iowa was still on a holy tear, and the Iowa media were having a field day. It was difficult not to notice a bevy of new Hawkeyes merchandise at the Southern Hills Mall in Sioux City. The Cornhusker T-shirts, jackets, and sweat pants that used to occupy prime retail space were now being relegated to the back of the store.

When Auburn University came to Memorial Stadium to play the unranked, 1-2 Huskers in early October, it was appropriate that it was raining to beat hell. As I listened to the game at the station, Lyell Bremser made mention that there was a huge crowd on hand. Who knew they'd get to witness a baptism?

Turner Gill trotted onto the field in the second quarter to muffled cheers and a buzz of anticipation. As was their recent custom, the Huskers had already fallen behind, managing to move the ball against the Tigers with some success but ultimately sputtering with Mauer at the controls. One of Mauer's third-down passes was closer to the student section than to NU tight end Jamie Williams. The boos started raining down.

For the previous two weeks, my dad had been screaming for Gill, a highly touted sophomore from Fort Worth, Texas. Turner was highly touted, it seemed, because he chose to come to Nebraska instead of Oklahoma and therefore symbolized all those things Oklahoma was and Nebraska didn't have the courage to be – slick, quick, daring. As Bremser announced his arrival into the Husker huddle, some members of the Smith's Standard crowd weren't in the consecration mood. They wondered, in tones laced with skepticism and latent racism, if Turner possessed the smarts to run Tom Osborne's offense.

Gill really didn't do anything messianic on that soggy Saturday. He left the game in the third quarter and came on again in the fourth. But as the game went on, the Huskers began to wake up – first they tied the game 3-3, then converted an Auburn turnover into a touchdown to take a 7-point lead into the final quarter. And you could feel that, with this kid running the show, something big was about to happen – something massive and still without form, though; you weren't sure what it was. Finally, with four minutes left in the game, you got your first glimpse.

Nebraska was at the Auburn 8, and Osborne called for a pass. Gill, who wore No. 12, retreated to throw but couldn't find anyone open. So he improvised. He pulled the ball down, slipped past a linebacker's reach, and ran through a hole in the Tiger defense for a touchdown.

Sounds simple enough. Plays like that happen in today's game so often that there's a term for it – *breaking containment*. But in 1981 in Lincoln, Nebraska, that type of play-making from the quarterback was mind-blowing. The final gun sounded, Nebraska was victorious, and relief washed over the state from border to border. The Cornhuskers were good again, so we were too. In the locker room, Osborne skillfully dodged questions about who would start under center the next week against Colorado, but it didn't matter. By sundown, when the highlights of Gill's run flashed across the TV news, we had already put our hands in the hand of the man who scored the touchdown.

The team was 2-2, but something was brewing. Gill had touched off some kind of tectonic movement, like the Reformation or the Renaissance. Whatever it was, you knew our Dark Ages were passing (or running, in this case). And what of Mark Mauer? In the euphoria of finally finding our Redeemer, we were feeling particularly generous. The hate mail he'd been getting would most certainly subside. And he could keep his scholarship, just as long as he stayed on the sideline.

Perfect

NEBRASKA 68, NEW MEXICO STATE 0 – SEPTEMBER 18, 1982

To say that Nebraska fans have high expectations is sort of like saying Rush Limbaugh tends to lean a tad right of center. Each year we expect the Huskers to pull down a preseason Top 10 ranking, win the conference, and challenge for the national championship. In other words, we expect them to be perfect, or darned close to it, each time they take the field.

Fans of other schools, or even Nebraskans who (gasp) aren't fervent followers of the Big Red, might think using perfection as a standard in regard to a bunch of oversized college students is unrealistic at best. To them I say: Bullcrap. We've seen perfection here before. The last time it rolled through town was 1995, when nobody came within two scores of the vicious grain thresher Osborne had assembled. Sure, in the back of our minds we suspect the untouchable 1995 team was probably the exception and not the rule, but that doesn't stop us from believing that each week we should see that same brand of utter dominance. This is why for good chunks of the football season, Nebraska fans are in genuinely foul moods: We know what perfection looks like in scarlet and cream, and we know it's possible. And when we don't see it, we get cranky.

You want to know what a "perfect" game is like? Let me tell you:

1. *The game is played at home during the daytime.* This should go without saying. Also, it helps if the weather is agreeable – say, 72 degrees with a light wind out of the northeast. I just made that up, but it sounds nice, don't you think? We get so few of these types of days in Nebraska and even fewer of them on a home Football Saturday.

2. *The outcome is quickly determined.* Ask Husker fans what their favorite victories are, and they'll immediately summon the 24-17 victory over Miami in the 1995 Orange Bowl, the 17-14 upset of top-ranked Oklahoma in 1978, and the legendary 35-31 triumph in the '71 Game of the Century. But those are their favorite *close* victories, ones that required fourth-quarter heroics on the field and some serious anxiety in the stands. So while those wins were immensely satisfying, they weren't particularly *comfortable* ones. And being comfortable is an important part of being a Husker fan. As the saying goes, Why bother putting away a team in the fourth quarter when you can do it in the first? Nebraskans like their games nice and neat and over within a few minutes of kickoff; if our boys quickly build a massive lead over an intimidated opponent, it means it's going to be an easy day for us too. The initial worry over the outcome can melt away and leave you to obsess about other, less obvious elements of the game – like whether we're substituting enough to build sufficient depth and experience at weakside linebacker or what the starting offensive lineup will look like two years from now based on the play of the young scrubs. You know, important stuff like that.

3. *As much Husker scoring as humanly possible.* Coaches have an unwritten rule that says once you've proven your team is vastly superior and you're ahead by, say, 35 points, you're supposed to let up on the gas and give the other team a sporting chance to make the contest respectable. We fans, however, believe merely beating Kansas 45-7 is a sign of weakness. If the score is, say, 52-0 with a minute to play,

there's still time to make it 59-0. Or, hell, 66-0, if we can recover our own onside kick and then throw deep. The bigger the score, the better we ultimately feel.

4. *The defense pitches a shutout.* There's nothing like a goose egg on the scoreboard to perpetuate the image of defensive impenetrability and strike fear into the hearts of future opponents. If a shutout isn't possible, one score is acceptable, assuming it's coming against the third- and fourth-string defenders. The point is to hold the opponent to single digits, thereby keeping the score sufficiently lopsided. Giving up more than 9 points can lead to questions about defensive depth. And if the game yields questions about perceived vulnerabilities, it can't be considered "perfect."

5. *The guest of honor gets some action.* On home Saturdays there's always a sign tacked up somewhere in Memorial Stadium from a place like Hershey, Brainard, or Imperial, lauding a homespun walk-on. This guy is usually buried deep on the depth chart and doesn't play much. Watching him trot onto the field, with NU up 49-0 and the Huskers' huddle getting more foot traffic than Grand Central Station, puts a sublime punctuation mark on the victory. Usually you can hear a faint buzz of approval coming from one corner of the stadium or another, which means a few people from his hometown have noticed his entry into the lineup. It's even better if he remembers his assignment and makes a tackle.

6. *The victory is achieved with the appropriate mathematical prowess.* This is perhaps the most important factor of all. As Nebraska fans, we find security and comfort in the numbers of the game – 260-some-odd straight sellouts, 42 consecutive non-losing seasons, 35 straight bowl appearances, three Heisman winners, 200-some-odd academic all-Americans – on and on the numbers go. The strength of Nebraska's program is its old-fashioned arithmetic. The perfect game requires four distinct numbers: 50 (points), 400 (offensive yards), 100 (players who get to see action), and 0 (major injuries). If the Huskers do that, everything else takes care of itself.

This is a daunting set of requirements. But like I said, we know that perfect storm is often within reach in Lincoln. It certainly was in 1982. Having already exacted brutal revenge by administering an opening-day five-touchdown flogging to the Iowa Hawkeyes, the Huskers were No. 3 in the major polls and had many of us believing this was Osborne's best team yet. Dr. Tom's sideline was so chock-full of talent, in fact, he had to draw up new formations to get all the stars on the field. Over the summer he created the weak set, a sort of off-set-I without the traditional lumbering fullback, so he could get Roger Craig and Mike Rozier into the same backfield behind Turner Gill, our all-everything signal caller.

The New Mexico State Aggies, on the other hand, were possibly the worst team in America. They arrived at Memorial Stadium in mid-September fully expecting to get crushed into a fine crimson powder. The poor souls knew they were here only because their athletic director struck one of those hey-come-up-to-Lincoln-and-let-us-pound-on-you-for-three-hours-and-we'll-write-you-a-big-fat-check-so-you-can-finally-buy-some-new-uniforms deals with Bob Devaney. The Vegas odds makers refused to establish a line on the game, it was such a mismatch.

We were looking for perfection on this bright and sunny day at Memorial Stadium, and we got it: The weather was perfect. The Huskers jumped to a big lead. They set an NCAA record for rushing yards and first downs. The defense didn't give up a single point. And Osborne played everybody who suited up.

Over the next two years, Nebraska and its high-powered offense would compile a 24-2 record and provide us with two of the best teams in school history. Yet during that magical stretch full of huge plays and inflated scores, there were really no other games that we could consider "perfect," at least not to the degree that we witnessed against the Aggies. It was a memorable contest, even if it was against an unmemorable foe. I turned off the radio that afternoon feeling satisfied and fulfilled, knowing that for once the Big Red had lived up to every one of our expectations – even exceeded a few of them.

Now that was a damn rare thing.

Are You There, God? It's Me, Steven

NEBRASKA 28, OKLAHOMA 24 – NOVEMBER 26, 1982

On Football Saturdays in Nebraska, Husker football is bigger than just about everything, including the Beatles. And they were bigger than Jesus, so you draw your own conclusions.

Notice, however, that I did not say Nebraska football is a religion. That notion is well past cliché, and it's far too easy to carry through:

Memorial Stadium is our cathedral, you say? And its bleachers are our pews? Ha ha, that's clever.

Still, it's not like there's no truth in the notion. The traditions, customs, and institutions surrounding Nebraska football possess a weird reverence, from the clapping-for-the-opponents thing to the communal concept of "Husker Nation" to the solemn retirees wandering around in "In the Deed the Glory" T-shirts. And like religion, Cornhusker football provides a sense of belonging for its followers. From Sunday through Friday, other Husker fans are just the distracted cashier, the woman whose dog takes a dump in your yard every night, or the jerk that cuts you off in traffic. But on Football Saturdays, these people are your brothers and sisters, and together you shall march side-by-side into battle to face the demons of the day (of course, it helps if those demons represent a school with "west" or "north central" in its name that can barely field a three-deep roster, but you get the idea).

It's true that there's a good dose of religion in football. There's the famous story of Bob Devaney declaring "even the Pope would vote us No. 1" following NU's Orange Bowl win over LSU on January 1, 1971. When he coached, Osborne regularly quoted scripture, like the time he summoned 2 Timothy 1:7 before the Huskers' emasculation of Florida in the '96 Fiesta Bowl. For years a regular game-ending sight was receivers' coach Ron Brown on one knee, leading players in prayer. Also, countless athletes over the years have celebrated big plays with quick salutations to the Guy Upstairs. So while we know Husker football isn't a religion, at times the lines can get a little blurry, which probably also explains why those "On the Eighth Day God Created the Cornhuskers" bumper stickers were so popular back in the '80s.

It might not be a faith in the official sense of the word, but being a Husker fan can lead you to question your own now and then. In 1982 I had to wonder what kind of god would allow us to get hosed by the referees at Penn State when it was obvious to every sentient being in the Milky Way that Mike McCloskey was out of bounds when he caught that last-second pass from Todd Blackledge to beat the Huskers. And what kind of deity would then toy with me by allowing the Nittany Lions to get clobbered the next week and fall behind Nebraska in the AP poll, only to permit them to leapfrog NU in the rankings a few weeks later after a televised win over Notre Dame?

Still, there was plenty to get excited about after Thanksgiving, when Oklahoma returned to Lincoln to play the Cornhuskers for the Big 8 title. The Huskers were 9-1 and again ranked third, with Gill at the wheel, commanding the nation's most potent offense. The Sooners were 8-2 and alive in the Big 8 race thanks to man-child running back Marcus Dupree. This guy, a freshman, was one of those extraordinary physical specimens who looked like he was assembled in a lab. He was fast and quick and built like a tree trunk. So while everyone agreed Nebraska had the better team, Dupree's mere presence negated any advantage the Huskers held.

Like I had two years earlier, I watched the game on TV with my mom. By now, however, she had taken to lying down for short naps ("snaps," she called them) whenever the game took a turn for the worse and she just couldn't bear to watch. For good long stretches, it was just me in the living room, lying on our orange-and-black shag carpet, hands on my chin, hoping the next play would finally be the one to get us on track.

That never entirely happened. The Cornhuskers started well, grabbing a fumble near midfield and punching it in a few plays later on a Gill scramble. But by early in the second quarter, the Sooners had ridden Dupree's punishing runs to a 10-7 lead.

I could feel that familiar panic setting in, so I got up and did what any right-minded Cornhusker fan would do. I climbed the stairs to my room, got down on my knees, and prayed. More accurately, I begged God to give the Cornhuskers a hand. I started bargaining: If he'd help the Blackshirts get a handle on Dupree, I'd stop fishing the quarters out of Dad's change dish so I could play video games at the bar downtown. If he would help Turner Gill hit open receivers and maybe even pitch the ball on the option, I'd tear up the *Playboy* some friends and I had found at the public bathroom at the park. If he could just . . .

"What are you doing?"

Mom was standing in the doorway. She had heard me bolt upstairs. When she asked again, I attempted in vain to convince her I was invoking the powers of the almighty to deal with something important, like world hunger or the civil war in Upper Volta. She looked unconvinced.

"Hmmm," she said, hands on her hips. "I see. Well, what about that little boy in Oklahoma who's praying right now for *his* team to win?"

Well, what about him? It wasn't my fault he chose to cheer for the Legion of Doom. However, realizing how stupid I must have looked appealing to the heavens for a Cornhusker victory, I figured silence was the best course of action. My mother motioned me toward her and said something about how God didn't have a rooting interest in football games. Shrugging, I followed her back to the living room.

No sooner did we settle back in front of the TV than Gill pivoted and flared a pass in the flat toward another flesh-and-bone mortal, Irving Fryar. The ball was low, though, and it skipped to Fryar on one bounce. No whistles blew. Fryar, still standing behind the line of scrimmage, wound up and flung a 37-yard strike to tight end Mitch Krenk. The Bounceroosky, as it would become known, gave the team the boost I was hoping for – moments later Doug Wilkening scored the first of his two second-quarter touchdowns, and Nebraska bolted into the lead.

Over the next two hours, I watched nervously as Nebraska bent but didn't break and held on for an inspired victory over the Sooners. As the red-dressed lunatics stormed the field and yanked down the goalposts, it suddenly sunk in: By virtue of defeating Oklahoma, NU had won its second straight conference title and had earned another trip to the Orange Bowl.

Shortly after the game ended, Mom turned her attention toward fixing supper. While she was distracted, I took the opportunity to head back upstairs to send up a quick thank you, just in case.

Acceptance

MIAMI 31, NEBRASKA 30 – JANUARY 2, 1984

Did you hate junior high? Don't answer that, silly, it's a rhetorical question. Of course you hated junior high – although you might have been hard-pressed to hate it as much as I did. In seventh grade, nearly all the other boys began to develop biceps and pectorals and other bulbous features. I did not. Not coincidentally, the girls suddenly seemed to forget my name. To compensate, I shrewdly developed nuclear-style acne and bad eyesight, which necessitated topical compounds that stunk of sulfur and eyeglasses from Sears. I also was confined to a metal body brace because I had scoliosis.

About the only route to acceptance in junior high was to be an athlete, but my brace severely limited things. I'd spent the past three years dreaming about becoming a quicksilver option quarterback in the mold of Turner Gill upon my arrival at Bancroft-Rosalie Junior High. Instead I was relegated to placekicking duties – a specialist, as the coach liked to say. There were, however, two small hurdles between me and actual playing time: 1) I didn't handle kickoffs because our starting quarterback, an impossibly athletic eighth-grader who was bigger than some high school seniors, could kick farther; and 2) we played eight-man ball, where the custom was to go for 2 points after a score. I spent the fall of 1983 on the sideline, clipboard in hand and decked out in ridiculously oversized football gear, helping the student managers with game statistics. Let me tell you, I could keep a mean stat in my day. But this did not once help me get a date for any school dances.

But there was one girl in my class who smiled at me regularly, usually laughed at my jokes, and didn't slide her chair away when she happened to be sitting next to me at lunch. With long brown hair and eyes to match, she generally associated with the popular crowd; I naturally assumed she was out of my league. Still, she seemed to be paying attention to me more than the other girls did, so I had to be sure. One day in September when she and I were in the school library alone, I summoned the courage to tell her I liked her. She giggled self-consciously, closed her notebook, and left, smiling to herself. I took this as a sign of encouragement. But by the end of the day, my declaration was all over the hallways. She had told everyone but the school janitor what I had said. People were stopping and laughing as I walked by, sputtering with laughter as they tried to say her name and mine in the same sentence. Turns out the little tart had been "going with" one of the starters on the football team for the past two weeks. I had spent most of that time memorizing Mike Rozier's yards-per-carry average; I hadn't noticed them smooching over by the fire escape during recess.

I trudged home by myself that day, convinced I was the biggest loser on the continent. I felt unsightly, uninteresting, and unattractive – on a scale of 1 to 10, my self-esteem was hovering around minus 36. I sighed and searched for anything that could possibly make me ever feel happiness again. And then I thought, *When Nebraska wins the national title this year, everything will be all right.*

I tell this story for two reasons. One, it should serve as a firm warning to all future middle school boys who may someday be looking for love in all the wrong places. If you're considering being honest about your feelings to a girl from a different social stratosphere than yours, for the love of Jesus, boy, don't do it. Two, it illustrates our state from a national perspective. If the United States were made up of fifty junior high kids, Nebraska would probably look and act a lot like how I was in the seventh grade – we might not have acne, bad glasses, or body braces, but for whatever reason, we can't seem to get out from under our border-to-border inferiority complex.

Maybe it's because we live smack in the middle of what people on the coasts cynically call "flyover country." Or maybe it's the notion that damn-near everything interesting seems to happen somewhere else. Or maybe it's because, as our buddies from Boulder like to point out, we have no big cities, no major in-state tourism, no beaches, no oceans, no mountains. We do have eyes, though, and we can see we live on a gigantic, dusty, flat, empty tabletop that's neither entirely Midwestern nor entirely part of the West. There's a reason it's called the Plains – it's ordinary and unexciting and featureless and not really worth a second look. So we suppose we have to be that way too.

The Chamber of Commerce presidents and rah-rah community boosters around the state would probably take issue with that characterization. But deep down they know a general lack of self-esteem exists here. It's subtle but noticeable. Strike up a conversation with a Nebraskan, and it won't be long before he or she starts to apologize for the state.

But we never, ever apologize for the football team. Therein lies our main source of hope and happiness, especially for those of us growing up in places other than Lincoln or Omaha. On Saturdays the rest of the state melts away, its shortcomings forgotten. All that exists is Memorial Stadium, and the Huskers' supremacy on the field makes all of us nobodies finally feel like somebodies. Set loose for one afternoon, we can finally bask in what's good about our state. And dammit, if the rest of the country would only stop boogie-boarding and going to Broadway shows and trying to catch glimpses of nubile movie actresses for a second and take a good look at us, they'd obviously see how good we are too.

And that, friends, was why the autumn of 1983 was so special. The Scoring Explosion – the moniker given to the Cornhuskers' hyperpotent offensive unit led by Turner Gill, Mike Rozier, and Irving Fryar –

had finally put enough points on the scoreboard to turn America's undivided attention toward us. Rightly tapped as the No. 1 team by both national polls to start the season, the Huskers unleashed an offense so mind-bogglingly powerful the Soviets wanted it covered under the SALT II treaty. After Nebraska bombed defending champ Penn State on national TV to start the season, Rozier graced *Sports Illustrated* beneath the headline "Oh, Those Huskers!"

That game started a surge of national media attention that latched onto Nebraska and never let up. After outrageous wins over Wyoming, Minnesota, UCLA, and Syracuse, *SI* wrote the words we already knew were true: The 1983 Nebraska Cornhuskers were destined to become the greatest college football team in history. Thus it was decreed, one full week before they started Big 8 play.

Autumn marched on, and our top-ranked team continued to win with basketball-like scores. In consecutive weeks, the Huskers scored 69, 51, 72, and 67 points, and before long we were smiling along with stories from *Time*, *USA Today*, and NBC's *Nightly News* that marveled at the passion of Husker fans – our sellout streak, our reverence for our coach, our single-minded constituency of support. Everything said, written, or broadcast about Nebraska – the team and the state – seemed to be golden. Our necks hurt from nodding along with all of the sunshiny coverage. It was a great time to be a Nebraskan.

By late November, after the Huskers had whipped Oklahoma for the third straight season – yawn, weren't these chumps once our big, bad archrivals? – we allowed ourselves to believe. Not hope, believe. And hey, why not? Rozier, on the strength of his blasting runs, powered himself to the top of the Heisman heap. The leviathan Dean Steinkuhler took home the Outland and the Lombardi, signifying he was far and away the nation's best lineman. The multifaceted Big Red offense – piloted by possibly the greatest quarterback in school history, Turner Gill – was overloaded with all-Americans and unanimous all-conference selections. They scored every eight times they snapped the football. The Orange Bowl in Miami against the upstart hometown university wasn't even going to be a game; it was going to be a coronation.

We were so busy basking in the limelight, in fact, that we ignored every single warning sign. We forgot that Miami's players also saw Time, USA Today, and NBC's Nightly News, and it slipped our minds that they were probably pinning up the articles referring to the Huskers as the greatest team of all time.

Then, about the time NU started practicing for the game, the most arctic weather in memory blasted the state – and stuck around. It was so hideously cold in December, in those pre–Cook Pavilion-indoor-practice-field days, that more than a few practices got canceled or shortened. In contrast, when the team arrived in Miami, south Florida was going through a stretch of nasty, Amazon-style heat and humidity. Sitting in the living room one night after Christmas, I listened to a sound byte on the radio of Tom Osborne saying that NU was having trouble getting used to the conditions. It apparently had no impact on me; I immediately went upstairs, drew up a "Nebraska – 1983 National Champions" poster on a sheet of typing paper, and taped it to the door to my room.

When the day of the game finally arrived, the cold spell in Nebraska abruptly ended. Temperatures in the state soared into the 40s. I spent that afternoon sweating under my snowsuit while building a fortress in my yard with melting snow. It felt like it was about 80, given that it had been so cold for so long. And I could only imagine what it must have been like for Nebraska's players down in Miami, where it was *really* 80 degrees. By the time our team stepped onto the sultry floor of the Orange Bowl that evening, Miami coach Howard Schnellenberger had whirled the hometown into a foaming frenzy, and the ambush was officially sprung.

Now, if you don't know what went down in that sweltering, sandy hellhole on January 2, 1984, you might want to stop reading right here. I'm stunned you've made it this deep into a book about the Nebraska Cornhuskers, quite frankly. For the record, though, the Hurricanes did not sit back and hope to just make it a good game. They attacked our terrifying juggernaut with abandon, not realizing the juggernaut was actually terrified. And Miami stole the game and the national championship when Tom Osborne, trailing 31-30 with forty-eight seconds left, eschewed kicking the extra point and went for 2 points, though he knew a tie would have put a mortal lock on his first national championship. On the ill-fated play, Gill rolled right and threw his final pass toward Jeff Smith. But the ball was tipped and fell harmlessly to the painted turf. Just like that, it was all over.

It's been said that that play call defined Tom Osborne's career.

Over the years his choice has been lauded in every daily newspaper in America. It's been talked about in the nation's biggest sports magazines and discussed on radio programs. That Orange Bowl has been shown and re-shown hundreds of times and has had thousands of words written about it. There are no adjectives left to describe it. But there are a few misconceptions still out there.

One mistaken belief is that when the sun came up the next day, every Nebraskan serenely put his hand over his heart and celebrated Osborne's decision, understanding fully that going for 2 was the honorable thing to do for a man of such impeccable integrity, class, and morals. This is merely sentimental bullshit. That school of thought, that Cult of Osborne, wouldn't become prevalent in Nebraska until more than a year later, when Dr. Tom published *More Than Winning* and let us in on his definition of success in football and in life. No, in the awful aftermath of the 50th Orange Bowl Classic, most of us were in shock. Three years in a row, three national title near-misses – first to Clemson, then to Penn State, then to the Miami-effing-Hurricanes, of all teams. And we started to wonder, What if this is Nebraska's destiny, to always have to play Goliath to some random team's David whenever they felt like stepping it up and showing a flash of brilliance once in a while? This simply wasn't fair.

But that was nothing compared to the feeling of abandonment that followed. Here we had been No. 1 all autumn long – king of the hill, top of the heap – and everyone had led us to believe they really, really liked us. Now, the story had moved. The nation's eyes had turned south, toward warmer climes, toward Schnellenberger and Bernie Kosar. It was suddenly as if none of us existed.

Fittingly, our Christmas break ended the day after the Orange Bowl. It was a challenge to get out of bed that morning; the game ended well after eleven, and I spent a good chunk of the night staring at my ceiling, too stunned to sleep. Worse, when morning came, I knew it would be time for me to return to the abyss that was seventh grade. For me and everyone else in red, as it turned out.

In All Kinds of Weather

NEBRASKA 49, IOWA STATE 0 – NOVEMBER 9, 1985

One of the most often repeated axioms from the Official Treasury of Hokey Cornhusker State Sayings is that if you don't like the weather in Nebraska, just wait five minutes. Because it'll change, see. Get it?

I know. It's about as funny as it is accurate. But I do understand the spirit of the saying. We've got a little bit of everything when it comes to weather. Sometimes the ceaseless heat and soul-crushing humidity makes you wonder exactly how you wound up inside your own oven. There are awful stretches of July and August that are so unmercifully hot the Firestones on pickup trucks actually melt onto the pavement, birds burst into flames in midair, and the populace starts having irrational thoughts, like considering trips to air-conditioned movie theaters for shows like *Daddy Day Care* and *Garfield: The Movie*. Crazy stuff like that.

Eventually, the heat breaks, and there are a lovely few weeks in October, a time we in Nebraska like to call "autumn." The humidity dissipates and you can wear a jacket and the trees turn colors and it's actually very pleasant. We spend this period furiously raking leaves, because we don't have a lot of time; soon enough, the switch will get flipped over to winter and the TV weathercasters will be warning about vertical jet streams and single-digit wind chills that only the Plains could whip up. And for the next several months, a bitter cold squats over the state that is just as vicious and cruel as the summer heat, and as you drag yourself to school through drifting snow, you think to yourself, *First chance I get, I'm moving to California.*

According to my father, who was always right by the way, it was good to see the seasons change. It built character, he said, and showed that everything in life was fleeting. Just to be argumentative, I would usually bring up the Nebraska offense's eternal propensity to run, run, and run some more as evidence to the contrary. And that's when Dad would look into his coffee mug, take a slow slurp, and announce it was time to go chop some firewood.

Another football-as-metaphor moment: Keeping the ball on the ground in autumn was as central to the Nebraska mindset as tilling

31

the ground in spring. And the style didn't just *fit* Nebraska, it *was* Nebraska. We're descendants of a bunch of burly frontiersmen, after all, and ramming the ball right at the opponent is our nod to their hardiness and discipline. The West Coast offense is nifty, sure, but our favorite games with that offense are still the ones where they run more than they pass. None of those little dinky-doo passes can fulfill us like the 34 Fullback Trap. Watching barrel-chested guys like Ken Kaelin and Micah Heibel thunder down the middle of the field straight toward the "Californians for Nebraska" sign behind the north goal posts provided us that primordial sense of being that non-Nebraskans can only place on such trivial things as falling in love or becoming parents for the first time.

This is what the pundits on ABC and ESPN never seemed to get. In their pregame documentaries about Husker fans (which always seemed to start, tritely enough, with a rustic image of an old barn in disrepair), they'd portray Nebraskans as a bunch of unedjumicated hilljacks who never seen hide-ner-hair of that newfangled forward lateral. Further, I can imagine that for national broadcasters like Brent Musburger, after years upon years of trying to make the same old toss-sweep toward the boundary sound new and interesting, the same-old, same-old from NU got a little tedious.

It's not like all of us watching or listening didn't often share that sentiment. For the love of Devaney, Tom, call a play-action pass, a crossing route, a screen . . . *anything* to mix it up! But those were only fleeting temptations; we knew on which side our bread was buttered. So when the national bobbleheads started in with the slights about NU being "one-dimensional" and "boring," we'd smile, nod, and accept the label, safe in the knowledge that the scoreboard usually agreed with our team's deep-seated squareness. We knew it wasn't flashy. But we watched and loved it anyway.

A running offense is also an all-weather vehicle, and in 1985 Nebraska definitely needed one. Field-level temperatures reached a come-on-that-can't-be-right 120 degrees during the season opener against Florida State. But by the time the Iowa State game arrived in November, winter had too. This game was memorable on several different fronts – first, I got to go because the two banks in Bancroft forked out for forty Husker tickets for the Bancroft-Rosalie High School football team; I'd given up placekicking long before my freshman year but I helped with the team enough to merit a trip to Lincoln. Second, we sat in ground-level metal bleachers along the southwest tunnel, and the Huskers strode right past us as they took the field; I popped Jim Skow's shoulder pads encouragingly as he passed by. Third, our bus driver almost left me in Lincoln after the game.

That last memory had something to do with how cold it was that day. And to be a Husker fan, you're going to have to do your share of element-braving. There's the intermittent cold – dry and sporadically gusty but nothing a good cap, coat, and Eddie Bauer socks can't handle. There's the soggy cold – wet and messy but easy to vanquish if you have a hooded windbreaker. There's the wintry, fluffy cold – when snow and wind blows in your face, but you can stymie it by dressing in layers and hitting your flask once a quarter. And then there was the cold that hit Lincoln, Nebraska, on November 9, 1985 – the meanest, harshest, cruelest, evilest, bitterest, most nerve-numbing cold I can ever remember. If that doesn't describe it well enough, try to imagine the reception Steve Pederson might get at a Solich family reunion.

It was even colder than that.

It didn't help, either, that we were facing north, right into the teeth of this nasty wind, in the middle of a giant wind tunnel. On the bus ride down, I wondered how it was possible for the Bancroft banks to get a block of forty tickets at Memorial Stadium so easily. Now I knew. They were the worst seats in the house, on one of the worst days in the house: With wind chill, it was a balmy 4 degrees.

Thing was, I don't remember really caring. I was keenly aware of how nasty it was, of course; I had bought four Runzas in the first half – two that I ate and two that I kept pressed against my face to keep warm. I even got a cup of hot coffee between quarters, and I didn't like coffee. But I certainly wasn't going to give up the seat and go back to the bus like some in our group. This was Nebraska football, man. People from small-town Nebraska didn't get chances to watch the team live and in person every day.

But even if I had season tickets and went to every game, I still would have sat through it to the end that day. *This was Nebraska football* – being cold was a necessary sacrifice to my fanaticism. In the years since, I've read how at Texas A&M some male undergrads put their hand in their pockets during the game and grab their family jewels as a sign of suffering along with the team. And I once saw stories about the sentries at the Tomb of the Unknown Soldier in Washington DC refusing to leave their posts as Hurricane Isabel rolled into town. When I hear these stories of duty, I can't help but think back to that freezing November day against Iowa State.

At the time I knew there was something foolish about sitting in the face of a punishing north wind and risking hypothermia, pneumonia, and other ailments ending in -*ia* just to watch the Cornhuskers run the same off-tackle play over and over. But there were also damn good reasons to do it, and those naturally won out. For one, when Jim Skow, the defensive tackle whose pads I had popped, broke through the ISU line and sacked Alex Espinoza for an 8-yard loss, he broke the great Willie Harper's record for yardage on tackles behind the line of scrimmage. I got to see that happen. And late in the second half I got my first in-person look at Steve Taylor, the much-heralded freshman from San Diego who was already being tabbed the next Turner Gill. I got to see that too. When Taylor scored on a simple 4-yard run in the fourth quarter, it was a thrill because of the hope he symbolized. I rose from my seat and yelled when he crossed the goal line; the bundled masses above me must've thought the same thing and let out their biggest roar yet.

When it was over, NU had nearly as many touchdowns (seven) as passing attempts (eight), and I was rightly satisfied with the Huskers' effort. They were keeping pace with Oklahoma in the race to represent the Big 8 in Miami and had a glorified scrimmage against the University of Kansas next week to tune up for the trip down to Norman. I stood up, feeling the blood flow return to my legs, and looked around our section of bleachers. It was virtually empty. I didn't recognize anybody; they were all gone.

I left the stadium, searching in vain for anyone I might know. Fans were pouring out of the exits, all in different shades of red, but my schoolmates were nowhere to be found. I could feel the air in my chest get heavy with panic. Maybe they'd headed back north at half-time – without me?

As I made my way toward the loop east of the stadium, though, I saw our bus, already warmed up and loaded, waiting for me. The head football coach was standing on a running board, looking out over the crowd in search of me. When we made eye contact, he impatiently waved me over. As it turned out, nearly everyone in our group had made their way back to the bus by the middle of the fourth quarter to get warm. They'd considered leaving to get a jump on traffic but realized they were one short.

People were pretty rankled at me, especially one senior who made it clear he needed to get home because he had a date that evening. Even though I couldn't feel my ears, I couldn't believe what I was hearing. Good grief, what kind of Husker fans were these people?

Shut Up and Play

OKLAHOMA 17, NEBRASKA 7 – NOVEMBER 21, 1987

Just 2:43 remained in the game, and what had been a bright and beautiful late-November day had turned deep and dark and cold. Steve Taylor, desperately trying to redeem himself and bring the Big Red back from the depths of hell, flung an ill-advised pass into coverage and had it picked off. And that's when we knew it was over, honest and for true. For the fourth straight year, the godless, outlaw Oklahoma Sooners had beaten us and were taking all the coveted spoils: the conference championship, the No. 1 ranking, and yet another trip to play in the Orange Bowl for the national title.

As their freshman quarterback, Charles Thompson, headed for the huddle to bleed the final minutes off the clock, Husker fans headed for the exits. One of them was so ticked off that he chucked his portable TV from the fortieth row of the north stands onto the Astroturf below, smashing it into a dozen pieces. That was pretty fitting. Undoubtedly, TV sets across the state were being either switched off or flipped over to reruns of *M*A*S*H* right about then. Me, I'd typically stay with the game until the very end regardless of the score, hoping for a miracle. Not this time. This time I hit the Off switch on our Quasar, hoofed it straight up to my room, and cranked up Whitesnake on my stereo. I was hoping the screeching guitar riffs would drive this catastrophe from my mind. In fact, I wanted to forget there was even a team called the Nebraska Cornhuskers. I was embarrassed to be associated with them.

All this didn't start with kickoff on Saturday. It began a week earlier, after top-ranked OU sputtered to a 17-13 win over Missouri. The Cornhuskers, see, had piano-wired Mizzou by five touchdowns earlier in the year, which had prompted all of the Comparative Score

Theorists around the state to compute how much better a team Nebraska was than OU. For those of you unfamiliar with Comparative Score Theory, the math goes something like this: If Team A beats Team B by 35 points and then Team C beats that same Team B by only 4 points, Team A is precisely 31 points better than Team C. See how simple and flawless that is? For years, legions of fans have taken this supreme logic to Las Vegas sports books, plunked down their sure wagers, and learned the hard way just why those casinos are so damn big. These are the same people who also swear by the *Farmer's Almanac* and who think they can drink all the Bud Light they like and not get fat.

Regardless, the pollsters bought into this same notion the week before the big game. After keeping OU atop the polls all season, they suddenly dropped the Sooners to No. 2 and replaced them with the Huskers. Then, in the middle of the week, word came that Jamelle Holieway, Oklahoma's jitterbugging quarterback (and the bane of our existence over the past two seasons), was injured and wouldn't play. The odds makers responded by making NU a 3-point favorite.

It made sense. The Big Red was leading the nation in total offense, thanks in large part to Taylor, who had established himself as one of the best players in college football. Defensive coordinators would play the pass, and Taylor would run for big yards. If they played the run, Taylor would pass – as he did against No. 3 UCLA when he fired a school-record five touchdown passes. The Blackshirts were similarly dominant, paced by future NFLers like Neil Smith, Brian Washington, and Broderick Thomas. The outspoken Thomas was one of the best outside linebackers in the college game at the time. Gifted with a nose for the football and terrifying lateral speed, No. 89 was a frequent visitor in opponents' backfields.

Broderick was a fan favorite because he was a favorite of the reporters. His stream-of-consciousness quotes continually provided a trail of sound bytes for even the laziest journalist to gobble up like a vacuum cleaner. It was through Broderick that we defined the 1987 campaign: It wasn't a schedule, it was a "hell raisin' tour"; it wasn't Memorial Stadium, it was "Our House." By November, as the wins by big scores continued to pile up, we were believing Tom Osborne had loosened the chains on his athletes just enough to finally find the synergy to win the national title. In 1983 Ozzie had the offense to win it but not the defense. In '84 it was the other way around. The 1987 team had firepower on both sides of the ball. Plus, it had some style. Week in and week out, the Huskers played with an almost unrecognizable verve and swagger.

Everything seemed to be pointing toward a Cornhusker victory. In addition to Holieway, OU's top fullback was also out injured. Even Barry Switzer, the old con man himself, was hobbling around on the sideline with a sprained knee. You could sense it in how the Huskers spoke and carried themselves as they awaited the Sooners' arrival in Lincoln – *Oklahoma can't play with us. It's not even going to be close.* We knew this to be true and so did Steve Taylor and Broderick Thomas, apparently. During a midweek press conference, they decided to say almost those exact words, out loud, in front of a dozen members of the media.

I don't remember the pronouncements changing my belief that NU would blast the Sooners at the end of the week, but the bold predictions gave me, for the first time in years, that same uneasy feeling I got when I watched Jarvis Redwine taunting that Oklahoma defender. Something wasn't right, but I couldn't quite place what.

Well, Taylor and Thomas turned out to be correct – the game wasn't even close. Oklahoma controlled the Cornhuskers from start to finish. The final score was 17-7, but it was never that close. The Huskers were outgained 2 to 1. OU held the ball for nearly forty minutes. The Sooners intercepted half as many passes as Taylor completed to his own receivers. If the Sooners hadn't fumbled so much, the score could have been 27-7 or 34-7 or even worse. The only NU player who seemed to suit up that afternoon was Henderson's John Kroeker, and ain't that a bad sign when your punter is your most valuable player? When all was said and done, more had been said than done.

In the week following the loss, we buried Taylor and Thomas on the call-in shows and letters to the Voice from the Grandstand. How dare they be so arrogant? I mean, *how dare they make us look bad?* In our anger, we seemed to have forgotten that we were saying the exact same thing during Oklahoma Week – *we're gonna blow 'em out.* It's just that no one with a microphone or notebook had asked us.

Broderick Thomas and Steve Taylor did some really amazing things during their time at Nebraska, but we've never fully absolved them for this game. A small part of us will always consider them brash, and Nebraska has never been a brash place. We've always been so ordinary, so Midwesternly old-fashioned, that any player we might suspect has an ego is automatically worthy of our caution. If we didn't know this before the so-called Game of the Century II, we certainly knew it afterward. We all had learned our lesson: Stick to the Husker way – commend the opponent before the game and clap for them as they leave the field, even if you don't believe for a minute they're worthy of your praise. That way we can take solace in the fact that if we have to lose, we can lose with dignity.

I filed this insight under "Too Little Too Late," right next to the realization that WrestleMania tickets don't make the best Mother's Day present. After four straight years of disaster and heartbreak at the hands of Oklahoma, I had finally lost all confidence Nebraska would ever make its way to a national title. I no longer believed. Sure, I had to acknowledge winning the title was possible, like peace in the Middle East or winning the lottery. And as the opening kickoff approached each fall I would be filled with new hope. But in the fan cache, hoping is a long way from believing, and deep down I knew Nebraska's window of opportunity had opened . . . and closed, without a title. If we couldn't win a championship with this team, it was never, ever going to happen.

Misery

NEBRASKA 26, MISSOURI 18 – OCTOBER 29, 1988

I was a bit different from everybody else in my teens, at least by small-town standards. I didn't hunt or play sports. I'd had problems with my curved spine long enough that they finally operated on it my freshman year of high school, and the procedure went badly. I spent the next two years recovering, and I've always felt cheated because of it, like I missed out on the crucial father-son rite-of-passage bonding sacraments such as shooting at wildlife or hitting the game-winning 3-pointer with him cheering me on.

Luckily, Dad and I had the Huskers. Talking about Steve Taylor and Ken Clark and Mike Croel and Todd Millikan gave us an important context in which we could share our testosterone. Before and after each game, while mowing the yard or raking leaves or sitting by our wood-burning stove, we would solve all of the team's problems. But even this common bond had its limits – we rarely if ever watched or listened to Nebraska games together. For Dad, Saturday was still a work day, so our discussions were either pregame conjecture or postgame meditation. We rarely got a chance to talk during the heat of the battle.

Even if Dad hadn't worked Saturdays, we wouldn't have gone to any games together. For one reason or another, he stopped attending athletic contests sometime around 1984. Maybe he developed agoraphobia. Or maybe he just tired quickly of loud, angry reactionaries and figured the last place he should go for peace of mind was Memorial Stadium.

A pair of tickets to the Nebraska-Missouri game landed in my lap in late October. I considered a chance to see the almighty Cornhuskers in the living, patsy-pounding flesh as a rare treat to be treasured and honored. I was so stoked about going, in fact, that I didn't care that the other ticket belonged to my mom, now part of the uncool crowd in my teenage mind. Or that she sprung them on me Friday night before the game as I was heading out to drive around and drink beer with my friends, which meant I needed to be home early so we could get going the next morning.

Like my curved spine, a decent-sized chunk of my game-day Huskerness I inherited from my mother. She was the one who was around the house on Saturdays; in the 1980s we probably watched or listened to a hundred games together. And no matter whom NU was playing, Mom was generally a nervous wreck. They could be five-touchdown favorites over Northwest Dogwater Tech, and she'd still expect the worst possible thing to happen. I picked up this tendency by osmosis. To this day I am always bursting with nervous energy on game day. I'm fidgety and over-talkative. I'm edgy and say things I shouldn't. All this because I'm absolutely certain that any second, something is going to go terribly wrong.

But taking our seats in the south stands before the game, we could detect an almost tranquil cheerfulness in the air. I got that feeling I had had during my first trip here – that everyone around us seemed to know everyone else, that they knew more about the game and the team than we did. Red-clad friends were laughing and chatting with their neighbors about the upcoming election, their kids' Halloween costumes, the weather – anything but the pending match-up on the field.

The serenity was due to the fact that Nebraska was a 39-point favorite over Missouri, who were wallowing through a quintessentially Missouri-like season at 2-4-1. Dr. Tom had given the obligatory midweek they're-a-lot-better-than-their-record-shows spiel, Osbornian for "we're going to wipe the dadgummed floors with these chumps," so there wasn't really anything to worry about.

But then the game started. Blitzing like madmen, the Tigers knocked out so many of Steve Taylor's teeth, he started to look like he was from, well, Missouri. Worse, they were separating him from the football and converting turnovers into points. You could tell it was going to be One of Those Days.

They say you learn the most about someone not when things are easy but when they're hard. Spend an afternoon at a stadium where the home team is playing like crap and then tell me you couldn't apply that to football fans too. The anger, indignation, and desperation are not pretty. And yes, this ugliness also exists at Nebraska. If anything it stands out even more in light of our reputation as "America's Classiest Fans." The best comparison to the fan transformation in Lincoln when something goes wrong is that scene in *Ghostbusters* where Egan and Venkman are tracking a ghost that looks like a harmless old librarian, but when they get too close she suddenly turns on them, wailing like a banshee, her face degenerating into a flaming skull. In fact, I was sitting right next to that woman on this particular day.

Fans cope with adversity in different ways. Some express their indignation at how the game on the field hasn't lived up to the one they've been playing in their minds. They start every sentence with "if only," like, "If only Ken Clark woulda held onto the ball, we'd-a got seven points out of that drive." Or, "If only Lorenzo Hicks coulda intercepted that pass that he got two fingers on while falling out of bounds with one second left, we'd-a had another three." And then they pause for a second before adding, ". . . dammit."

Some find comfort in facts and figures, summoning them as assurance that things could be worse. I was sitting next to one of these fans at halftime. The Husker offense had racked up all of 17 yards, and the boos had started. I tried to commiserate with him by saying how the Big Red attack had probably never looked this inept. He looked at me like I had just farted in church and said: "Oklahoma State, 1983." Then he rolled his eyes as if to say, *Duh, everybody should remember that.* He was right, they should.

But the most common reaction is to allow one's head to explode, to get really angry and act like a child. And we allow them to. The collective mental age of a football crowd is somewhere between nine and twelve, and Memorial Stadium is probably the only public place in Nebraska where it's perfectly acceptable to repeatedly yell "YOU STUPID IDIOT!" without fear of getting kicked in the groin.

Anger turned to outrage in the third quarter, with Nebraska having finally scored to make it 9-7. The Huskers kicked off, and on the return, defensive back Charles Fryar snatched a fumble in midair and ran it back for what appeared to be the go-ahead score. But the touchdown was nullified when LeRoy Etienne got hit with a personal foul away from the play. At that point, the stadium filled with language so uniquely and eloquently profane that the regulars at Smith's Standard Station would have blushed with envy.

Meanwhile, Mom and I were anxiously clinging to our final hope: Tom Osborne. We had learned through such objective media outlets as *Huskers Illustrated* magazine that Osborne was a legendary producer of in-game adjustments, and we hung what optimism we had left on Tom cracking the Tigers' defensive code. At some point during the third quarter, it began to happen: NU finally began to break off big plays against gambling Mizzou. The Blackshirts also were creating turnovers, and NU had turned the tide. Chris Drennan's field goal gave them a 2-point lead going into the fourth quarter, downgrading the mood in the stands from outright anger to a sort of hushed, glowering disgruntlement.

The fourth quarter was spectacular. Nebraska briefly relinquished the lead but then marched down the field on one of those inspiring drives that makes you want to hug a complete stranger. Fullback Bryan Carpenter busted a decent run, Ken Clark picked up a few more, and Steve Taylor zipped a pass to Morgan Gregory at midfield. One play later, Taylor put the ball in Carpenter's belly on the "read" option – where the quarterback, based on the defensive alignment, chooses to either run wide or hand it off straight up the gut. And Carpenter sailed, untouched, 49 yards for the winning touchdown. We stood and shouted for the final five minutes, as NU turned back a couple of Tiger drives to win 26-18 and stay unbeaten in the conference. When the clock hit zeroes, I was awash with exhilaration – what a stirring victory, what an inspired comeback, what a classic Missouri-Nebraska donnybrook.

Memorial Stadium greeted the final gun with a smattering of cheers and a lot of head shaking. The factoid savant next to me was already remarking to his wife that all these late-game heroics came against a team that was now 2-5-1. Two rows down, a scowling retiree abruptly grabbed his customized seat cushion and bellowed, "If they play like this against Oklahoma, they'll get their asses whipped!" As we moved down the aisle, the ramp and out of the stadium, it was clear this win was accompanied not by joy but by a sullen discontent. I don't know if Missouri considered the loss on the scoreboard a moral victory, but apparently we had decided it was a moral defeat.

I hated the fact that these people were bagging on *my* team. But then again, I thought, the Cornhuskers also belonged to them – probably moreso since they were season ticket holders. They knew the routine; perhaps they knew something I didn't.

When we got home it was well past dark, and Dad greeted us from his recliner. Before long he asked me about Missouri's blitz and said it reminded him of the attack the Tigers used back in 1981, when Turner Gill and Co. escaped with a dramatic 6-0 victory in Columbia. I laughed and said that thought had crossed my mind at least twice in the second quarter. Dad and I spent the next few hours talking about the finer points of the "read" option and how it was really the best play to run against a defense that was blitzing like Mizzou was. It was bound to break for big yards sooner or later, he said. NU just needed to keep running it. "It was a good, close game," Dad said. "That'll keep 'em honest." I wholeheartedly concurred.

I enjoyed our postgame talk almost as much as I did the last few minutes of the actual game. Maybe the old man was onto something by not spending too much time up in the stands. I mean, there's not a bad seat in all of Memorial Stadium, but that doesn't necessarily mean you could see things any more clearly.

Moving On

I'll tell you exactly what the 1989 Orange Bowl was about. It was about four hours long. And that was just too much time for me to sit and watch the Huskers get their manhood stripped from them on national TV by a vastly superior club. So, I did something I'd never done before when Nebraska was on TV: I turned the game off at half-time. I was so bored and fed up with the hegemony Miami had accomplished in the game that the only thing left to do was run. I called my friend Tim Flock, and together we barreled out to a kegger at a farmhouse north of Bancroft, where we eventually met up with our girlfriends.

More than anything, I wanted to surround myself with people who didn't identify as much as I did with the Cornhuskers. Fun-loving people my age who would be listening to z-92 on the radio, not dour old cranks tuning into Kent Pavelka on KFAB. Hopefully they'd form a warm amniotic sac around me and help me to forget that some fifteen hundred miles away, down on the sandy, godforsaken turf of the Orange Bowl, Steve Taylor was running for his life and losing, getting ridden face-first into the ground by lightning-quick defensive linemen.

Between a few gallons of Bud Light, a couple games of Speed Quarters, and a makeout session with my girlfriend, I accomplished that lofty goal. But even as the alcohol wrapped itself around my brain and everything became either funny or fuzzy, I quietly recognized all this was just a temporary fix, a trick I was pulling on myself to soften the blow I'd take the next morning when sobriety returned. Then it would be just me, the sports section, and that feeling of emptiness, bitter disappointment, and worry that followed a Husker loss.

But when the next morning did come, an odd thing happened. Bleary-eyed and hung over, I got up earlier than I should have, picked up the newspaper from the dining room table, and reflexively flipped inside, looking for the coverage of the game. Apparently, my dad had already gotten to the sports section. I considered looking around but instead I thought, The hell with it. I climbed back up the stairs and crawled back into my bed, which was still warm. My hair smelled like a combination of cigarette smoke and my girlfriend's perfume, and flashes of the evening came rushing back. What a good time I'd had, all because I had cut the Huskers loose a bit.

It felt good, liberating. I resolved to make a habit of it. I'd take down my Blackshirts poster and put up Guns N' Roses instead. I'd wear clothes made by Pepe and Guess and Bugle Boy instead of Champion and Russell Athletic. I'd stop referring to the team as "we." Hey, it couldn't be that hard – I didn't need the Big Red as much as I once did, after all. My senior year was heating up, my social calendar was bursting with activity, my love life was in full bloom, and I would be leaving for college in eight short months. It was time to clear out some room for more important things than my suspicions that the option offense was outdated, that Dr. Tom's recruiting base was shrinking, and that the Nebraska Cornhuskers were slipping from their spot among the nation's elite.

It was folly, I reasoned, to place so much of my self-esteem in the hands of a bunch of college jocks. Good grief, even if the Big Red had discovered a magical way to have beaten that Miami Pound Machine down at the Orange Bowl, I *personally* would not have done anything tangible to have helped them do it. Over the years, through countless Husker victories, the glory had always been theirs, not mine. I had only been basking in a reflection of it. I certainly wasn't going to get that close again, especially now that they were fading in the race for No. 1. I'd remain a fan, sure, like the way I was a fan of comic books and action movies maybe. But I wasn't going to be a fanatic anymore.

University

What Not to Wear

OK, so my nonfanaticism only lasted about six months. In June *Athlon's Big Eight Preview Magazine* hit newsstands and picked the Huskers to win the league. Then at my UNL freshman orientation, I was offered season football tickets. Opening day against Northern Illinois was right around the corner, the Big Red was ranked No. 4 in the country, and I could feel the hope creeping back in, like it always did in August.

And just in time too. I needed to get some new school clothes. One afternoon I went to Sioux City and bought a bunch of Husker gear – one red-and-white shirt for every day of the week, in fact. I thought this was a matter of obligation; like countless hicks from the sticks, I assumed everyone in Lincoln wore Husker gear all the time. Had I visited the Star City on a day other than a Football Saturday, I might have found out otherwise, but I hadn't.

Even now you can spot small-towners a block away on any given day in downtown Lincoln. They'll be wandering down P Street, craning their necks up at the Embassy Suites or standing inside the doorway at Chipotle Mexican Grill, fully transfixed by what must appear to be the most indecipherable menu they've ever happened upon. And they're always bedecked in bright red Husker apparel, as if they've decided to arrive four months early for the season opener. Another telltale sign is the quizzical look they have on their faces, like they're asking themselves, *Where are all the Nebraskans at?* I want to walk up to them and tell them I feel their pain, that I've been there before, and that it would be perfectly fine for them to wear their Old Navy flag T-shirts the next time they come to town.

That's not to say wearing red is a sign of ignorance or myopia. I fully recognize part of being a Nebraskan means dressing in team colors and visibly proclaiming your devotion to all things Cornhusker. A good Nebraska shirt can be both a flag and a badge of honor. It can denote your lifetime membership in our ever-expanding club. And unlike the paraphernalia put out by some schools, Husker gear is wholly representational and completely visceral. There's really nothing left to ponder about the person who wears it. What you see – "I am a Husker" – is what you get. That's something you can't say about the posers walking around in Michigan and Notre Dame gear, or worse, brand-new replica jerseys of the most recent national champion. The statement is poetic in its simplicity.

Witnessing all of that sentiment around you in Memorial Stadium can be an overwhelming and marvelous thing. That's what struck me when NU hosted Northern Illinois to open the 1989 season. That, and the sudden variety of ways people were proclaiming allegiance to NU – shirts, tanktops, ball caps, sweat suits, pullovers, windbreakers, headbands, fuzzy tam-o'-shanters. What's funny is that by today's standards, the variety of Husker gear I saw back then probably wasn't all that diverse. This was, after all, before Bill Byrne came to town and pushed the Husker merchandising machine into hyperdrive.

The amount of Husker gear available to fans has simply exploded, and that's not necessarily a good development. Walk into Husker Headquarters on P Street if you need an illustration. The value of the merchandise in the place rivals the gross national product of a small nation, because everyone with a silk-screen printer is now in the sports apparel business. And like it did with major league baseball, expansion has watered down the quality of the product. To wade through the Husker section of a store today is to drink in vatfuls of unabashed gaudiness: caps with a pissed-off corncob putting up his dukes, sweatshirts with logos commemorating the 2003 Troy State game as if it were the Game of the Century, tanktops with quotes from the defensive coordinator, T-shirts emblazoned with "Lincoln: A Beer Drinkin' Town with a Football Problem." It goes on like this forever.

It can be a lot to wade through and definitely overwhelming. Here, then, are some quick tips for game-day decorum:

1. *Wear the cap the right way.* A bill-forward ball cap is really the only acceptable game-day headwear. The whole sun visor thing was just a trend, the Eminem-style stocking cap is too thuggish, and anyone over ten who wears a foam cornhead to the game is precisely one-eighth of a man.

2. *Be advised the official color of the University of Nebraska-Lincoln is Pantone Red No.* 186. Chances are you have nothing that matches this exact color. In fact, chances are you don't even have two pieces of red gear that match each other. So don't bother trying. Unless you

want to look like you got dressed in the dark, wearing red on red is a bad idea.

3. *Don't wear identical outfits.* For God's sake, people, a thousand times, no. It might be tempting when you see a pair of Starter jackets marked down 50 percent to think, "Hey, why not one for me and one for the wife?" Well, let me ask you this: Have you heard the theory about how the longer couples are married, the more they start to look like each other? Why would you actually want to *help* that process along?

4. *Minimize the badass black.* The notion of black as a third school color came of age in the roaring Bill Byrne '90s. That's when, you may recall, the similarly hued Chicago Bulls were running circles around the rest of the NBA. That was then, this is now. The last I checked, the Bulls were 22-60 and out of the playoffs for the gazillionth straight year. Besides, we already stole that Alan Parsons Project song from them to use as our entrance theme. Isn't that enough?

5. *Don't desecrate the hallowed name.* There are acceptable places for the words *Nebraska, Cornhuskers,* and *Huskers* to be printed on game-day clothing – to wit, the front of a shirt, the back of a shirt, and the front of a baseball cap. Nowhere does it say, ladies, that it's OK to stamp it across your ass.

6. *Buy clothes that are big enough.* The sizes XL, XXL, and XXXL are now being offered at many of the establishments that peddle Husker goods. You may want to supersize your orders from these places from now on.

7. *Respect the statute of limitations.* The acceptable shelf-life of commemorative championship gear is ten years. After that the people wearing it start to look sad and desperate. It's time to move on; even the cast of *Friends* called it quits after a decade. I love my 1994 National Champions hat as if it were my own child, but it'll never see the light of day again.

8. *Don't mix gear.* It's unacceptable to root for Nebraska simultaneously with another school. Donning a Husker shirt along with, say, a Florida State cap is bordering on sacrilege. Stop hedging your bets and pick a side. This also applies to allegiances to professional teams: It's really nifty that you're a Husker fan *and* a Minnesota Vikings fan, but when you wear a red NU cap and a Vikes T-shirt, you look like the inspiration for that "When I Am an Old Woman, I Shall Wear Purple" poem.

9. *Don't compound the effect of wearing red polyester pants by putting on a white belt.* Or white cowboy boots, for that matter.

10. *Leave the smack shirts at home.* T-shirts that belittle the opponent are emblematic of the most vile kind of fan, just as "Stop Tailgating or I'll Flick a Booger on Your Windshield" bumper stickers signify the worst drivers on the road. They make you look oafish and simple and cocky and set you up for all kinds of justified ridicule if the results on the field don't go your way.

When Nebraska hosted woeful Northern Illinois, the game was tied 17-17 at halftime, but luckily the Big Red pulled away in the third quarter and won 48-17. If it had gone the other way, it wouldn't have mattered what we Husker fans would have worn that day – we all would have looked pretty silly.

Higher Learning

NEBRASKA 51, KANSAS 14 – NOVEMBER 11, 1989

The thing I liked best about college, other than being able to eat Pop Tarts for lunch, was being able to buy into the romantic notion that through hard work and perseverance I could help change the world. College was all about making a difference – and I did my part, by golly. I attended every home football game of the 1989 season and converted the disinterested kid next to me into a rabid Husker fan.

I met Dewey at the season opener against Northern Illinois. I'd gotten a student season ticket in the east stands, twenty-one rows up around the 30-yard line, just north of the band, and the first person I met as I arrived at my seat was a spitting image of a teen-aged Larry Mondello from *Leave It to Beaver.* He was sitting with his hands in his pockets, absent any red clothing and wearing a hat with "Montana" on it. As I slid past him to my spot in the stands, I asked him if he knew exactly what state he was in. That made him laugh, and we struck up a conversation while awaiting kickoff. As it turned out, Dewey was the son of a rancher near Missoula and was in Lincoln studying animal science. He had made his way to the football game because his dad, who had once spent a summer in Nebraska, had suggested he get a season ticket. Dewey confessed he had never been a big sports fan, knew very little about the Cornhuskers, and had even considered selling his ticket. But he decided to show up once and see what the big deal was.

What a peculiar individual, I thought. I had assumed anyone who stepped inside Memorial Stadium came from one of two distinct backgrounds. Either they grew up in Nebraska and inherited a powerful, inborn connection to the Cornhuskers or they grew up outside Nebraska with parents who once lived here and so were obligated upon threat of disownment to root for the team. Dewey wasn't in either camp. He was just here because he had nothing better to do and thought it might be a good time.

Well, there were seven home games scheduled that year, time enough to educate Dewey in the finer points of Huskerdom. We started simple, discussing how the Blackshirts got their name. But before long we were clipping through Bob Devaney's legacy, Tom Osborne's philosophy, and eventually, the deceptive simplicity of the multiple-option offense. By the end of the year, Dewey was calling out crack-back blocks, evoking players' nicknames – Gerry "Scrap Iron" Gdowski, Leodis "Mookie" Flowers – and booing the officials.

Yes, we booed the officials. Nebraska was playing Kansas, just a week after NU had dropped a 27-21 heartbreaker to the Colorado Buffaloes on the road. The loss had wrenched the Big 8 championship away from Lincoln and relocated it to Boulder, and in the wake of this unholy development every Nebraskan had placed the blame on the officiating crew. Colorado's win had nothing to do with the fact that Bill McCartney had been assembling a powerhouse at Folsom Field for nearly a decade and his wildly talented '89 team was the zenith of all he had built. Nope, in our minds it had *everything* to do with a pass-interference call on Tahaun Lewis that wiped out a key NU interception and allowed Colorado to score the game-winning touchdown two plays later.

Before the Kansas game (Nebraska always seemed to play Kansas the week after a tough loss) word circulated that the same bungling officiating crew would be in Lincoln that Saturday. So, when the zebras came onto the field, Dewey and I, along with what seemed to be the whole of Memorial Stadium, really let those bastards have it. And, man, did that feel good. Indignation is *such* a crucial element of being a Husker fan, and no one – players, coaches, officials – is safe from our righteous anger.

51

We like to pretend we're above that type of conduct, but I've sat in all four corners of Memorial Stadium over the years, and when the stadium rings with boos, it's never just the students. They get blamed, though, because of their section's reputation for being raucous. The student section most certainly is the loudest part of the stadium, and most everyone stands and yells the whole time. It's the home of rowdy cheers, plastic-cup fights, orange throwing, and loads of game-day spirit – figuratively and literally. Few students sit in their assigned seats, and if they do they bring along an extra friend or three. It's not neat and orderly and subdued, and there's certainly more fun going on in there than anywhere else in the stadium. The student section is easily the most identifiable society within the Memorial Stadium culture, which probably explains why it gets held responsible whenever red-clad fans misbehave. Blaming it on the students absolves the bankers, farmers, and insurance salespeople of making the entire state of Nebraska look bad. We see ourselves as a good and reasonable people, and if we can't ignore that we are capable of booing, then we'll confine it: *It's just the students, and they're not True Husker Fans.* It's a trick we play on ourselves that never gets old.

What seems to be forgotten in the who's-a-True-Fan debate is that Nebraska football is a plebian addiction as well as a patrician virtue, and we all have legitimate claims in the Big Red. We all assert ownership, whether we're CEO of a large Omaha company or a sophomore psychology major from Dorchester. Who owns the team more? The codger who talks about the rough-and-tumble days in the knothole section and who has sat in the same seat since Bill Jennings was walking the sidelines? Or the goateed mid-lifer who drives a red Ford F150 with NO1HSKR vanity plates but makes it to maybe one game every other year? Or is it the student whose tuition dollars go toward the university the football team supposedly represents? The answer, I imagine, is a tie on all counts. And by that virtue, Dewey, who didn't know Kenny Clark from Clark Kent, had just as much reason to be there, and to behave as he saw fit, as anybody else.

The student section, by and large, is the least obsessive section of Memorial Stadium. In other words, the students allow themselves to have fun, socialize, and recognize how much of the game of football is downright funny. In the first quarter against Kansas, Nebraska was up 16-7 after registering a safety. When the Jayhawks' punter came out for the ensuing free kick, he shanked it out of bounds and was hit with a 5-yard penalty. On the re-kick, he booted it out of bounds again and had to do it one more time from his own 10. The punter was clearly nervous now, and you could see him take a deep breath before putting foot into football for a third time. Sure enough, that kick, too, dribbled out of bounds, meaning the free kick would have to come from the KU 5-yard line. When the poor schlub finally got one to stay in bounds, Richard Bell scooped it up and jetted the ball back to the Jayhawk 30. To Dewey and me and the rest of the student section, it was really funny, and we had no trouble showing it. We pointed, we laughed, we guffawed. But the Real Husker Fans met the development with a buzz of urgency, as if this were a crucial point in the game (to be honest, I don't think there's been very many crucial points in Nebraska-Kansas games over the past thirty-five years, except maybe the coin toss). Apparently, True Fans don't think anything about Nebraska football is remotely humorous. They're too busy projecting their unhappiness and worry onto the field.

Dewey didn't make it to the season finale against Oklahoma. That showdown, which Nebraska ended up winning in a rout, was during Thanksgiving break, and he headed back to Montana to see his family. So I never saw him again after the victory over Kansas. Not even walking around on campus. I have no idea if he finished school or ever went to another Husker game. But we both got something out of being neighbors in the student section our freshman year. He learned the difference between the Power-I and the Ace Set, and I had found another compelling reason to attend Cornhusker games: They were fun.

Who knew?

Reality

COLORADO 27, NEBRASKA 12 - NOVEMBER 3, 1990

It goes without saying that most Nebraskans are conservative. The state has long been a bastion for the GOP and has handed its electoral votes to the candidate with an *R* behind his name in every presidential election since 1964. Conservative politicians hold dominion over everything from the statehouse to local weed control. The only interesting elections around here are the May primaries, when Republicans run against one another to determine who gets to butcher whoever the Democrats put up in November. Even the progressive-type thinkers in Nebraska define themselves as "centrists" and "moderates" because they're afraid if they use the "L word," they'll be hunted down by dogs. It's tough to be a liberal in the Cornhusker State when the common sentiment is that your ideology is responsible for everything wrong with the world, including crime, inflation, lousy public schools, and ESPN's increased coverage of professional soccer.

This is why it was unsettling to see a bunch of tree-hugging leftists assume command of the Big 8 Conference. The Colorado Buffaloes won the league outright in 1989. While NU foundered at the Fiesta Bowl, the Buffs became media darlings and played for the national championship. For right-leaning and (supposedly) right-thinking Nebraskans, this left-wing power grab was almost as big a travesty as Kennedy snatching the 1960 election away from Dick Nixon. And like that electoral boondoggle, there was something shady about how Colorado came to authority, though we weren't exactly sure what yet. However, we were quite certain that it couldn't be good for any of us.

The notion that Buffalo fans are a stadium full of baby-killing, gun-controlling, welfare-loving, Che-worshipping socialists is still widespread in Nebraska. I assume it's because the University of Colorado is in Boulder, which, like most college towns not named Lincoln, is largely liberal. Boulder is similar to, say, Iowa City in terms of its progressive climate, yet I've never heard a Cornhusker fan talk of the Hawkeyes' fan base as a bunch of bleeding-heart liberals. Which is odd, considering Iowa is traditionally a Blue State – that is, Democrats usually win it on election day. Colorado, on the other hand, has been a right-leaning Red State for decades. The difference in perception must be rooted in the schedule: We don't play Iowa every year, but we are at perpetual war with the Buffaloes. So we must demonize everything associated with them, and that means their fans must all be left-wing loonies. I've been to plenty Nebraska-Colorado games; I have a sneaking suspicion the mullet-headed dinks who cheer for CU occupy the same general spot on the political spectrum as the mullet-headed dinks who cheer for the Huskers, but hey, whatever it takes to make us feel morally superior.

Thing is, CU's supporters really don't need any help in being unlikable. By and large they're a bunch of ostentatious, Hummer-driving jerks, which made the Buffs' rise to power all the more troubling to us Plains folk. College football has long been more appreciated by

small states like Nebraska and Oklahoma, which don't have professional franchises to dilute the fan base – or worse, inject it with the
same breed of fans that makes up NFL crowds. The Buffaloes, by virtue of their location amid the Denver metroplex, drew this breed of
wicked fan in droves. These nouveau riche charlatans were the in-
sidious type who got more enjoyment from the other team's loss
than their own team's win. When Colorado beat NU in Boulder in
'89, testimonials about how badly our red-dressed clan of septuage-
narians was treated filled the local opinion pages. So by the time the
rematch in Lincoln rolled around in 1990, the battle lines had been
drawn, and the match-up's social significance was clear.

The Huskers weren't the only ones making headlines that autumn.
The Nebraska-Colorado game was to be played four days before the
general election, and the biggest ballot issue besides the race for governor was an initiative to cap yearly increases in government spending at 2 percent. The proposal was tailor-made to appeal to good ol'
Nebraska conservatism; in late August the state appeared ready to
support it. But then nearly every government-related interest rose up
against it, including Tom Osborne, who said such a spending lid
would hurt students' quality of life. It marked the first time, but not
the last, Osborne would cross over into politics and the first time, but
not the last, the state's voters would shrug and say, "Heck, if Coach
thinks it's a bad idea, I do too." We probably should have guessed that
in a decade's time, he would run for – and easily win – a seat in the
U.S. House of Representatives. Go for two, indeed.

Of course, Husker football and homeland were connected long
before Dr. Tom became Rep. Tom. And politicians have frequently
tried to take advantage of those links. It's no wonder many of the
campaign signs for state races in Nebraska sport red as a dominant
color. In his run for governor in 1998, Bill Hoppner even created a
campaign motif that mimicked the Huskers' script logo. And in an
election year, you can always find field workers hawking campaign
paraphernalia outside Memorial Stadium. As my friend Chuck and I
jogged toward Memorial Stadium in the sleet the afternoon of November 3, representatives from nearly every state and local political
campaign bombarded us with freebies: *Here, have a Kay Orr sticker.
Here, read this position paper from Jim Exon. Here, would you like a
Ben Nelson button? Here . . . here . . . here . . .* but the thing I wanted
wasn't *here,* it was over *there,* past the rows of field staffers and with

seventy-six thousand of my closest friends inside. Political campaigns were the last thing on my mind; the college football campaign
was first.

At that point the unbeaten Cornhuskers were in a three-way public-relations war with Virginia and Notre Dame for the No. 1 spot
and were about to go on TV to make their case to the nation that they
were the best team in all the land. Meantime, Colorado was 7-1-1 and
ranked ninth. Before leaving for the stadium, Chuck and I watched
an ESPN interview with Bob Devaney, who was clearly pitching the
Big Red for the top spot. "If we beat Colorado today, there's no doubt
we should be voted No. 1," the athletic director pronounced. It didn't
exactly have the noble timbre of "In the Deed the Glory," but these
were important times that called for drastic measures.

Such conjecture is necessary in college football, which is equal
parts athletic competition and political campaign. The absence of a
playoff means the teams make their case to the voters every Saturday
and then await the returns from around the country. With much of
their fate left up to voters, the coaches and players have to stump for
their teams after wins. Penn State's Joe Paterno did it in '82 on behalf
of his one-loss Nittany Lions, who needed some generosity from the
pollsters to leap-frog unbeaten Southern Methodist and give JoePa
inside position to eventually win his first national title. It can even
happen after losses: Who can forget teary-eyed Matt Frier of Florida
State in 1993, moments after the Fighting Irish had knocked off his
No. 1 Seminoles, literally begging the voters for another chance?
There's a reason the National Collegiate Athletic Association has
never officially recognized a national football champion: There's
never really been one. There are teams that have been unanimously
perceived as the best team in the nation at the end of the year by the
coaches and the sportswriters, of course, but in the NCAA's reality, the
mythical national championship is just that – mythical.

Through eight games in '90, Nebraska appeared at first glance to
be a great team. Our boys had racked up a string of impressive victories – but a closer look begged the question, Against whom? Quarterback Mickey Joseph, who we'd all hoped would be the next Turner
Gill, could run like a deer (but threw like one too, as the joke went).
Joseph had juked through defenses all fall, but those defenders had
played for the likes of Northern Illinois, Iowa State, Minnesota, and
Oregon State. The Buffaloes, on the other hand, had already battled

Tennessee, Illinois, Stanford, and Oklahoma. CU would be the only ranked team the Huskers would play during the regular season. Judgment Day was at hand.

It was an emotional game, as Senior Days always are. At the last home game of the year, those in their final season of eligibility are introduced, get a man-hug from the coach, and are greeted by cheers from the Memorial Stadium crowd. The introduction of defensive end Kenny Walker, who had been deaf since childhood, was particularly sublime: In the week leading up to the game, instructions had appeared in various media on how to salute No. 57 with silent applause – a sign-language clap in which you raise your palms high and then rotate them back and forth. To see every fan in Memorial Stadium, bundled from head to toe and making the motion in unison, was an inspiring sight.

Even more inspiring, though, was that Walker played like a madman that day. The all-American sacked CU quarterback Darian Hagan twice and regularly disrupted the Colorado offense. Meantime, Joseph and Co. found it tough sledding against the Buffaloes' thuggish defense, but Colorado turned the ball over a couple times, and the Blackshirts bent but did not break. By halftime the Cornhuskers had squeaked out a 6-0 lead.

It looked like our break finally came in the third quarter. Joseph pivoted on the option and sprinted around the right side of the Cornhusker line, as we'd seen him do so many times that autumn. It was a play CU had been stopping regularly, but this time, Mickey caught the corner, cut back slightly to his left, then bolted past the Buffalo defense down the west sideline, 48 yards and into the end zone standing up. Soggy from the freezing rain, Chuck and I and the rest of the stadium leaped from our seats and roared. One official raised his hands over his head and then another. But something was wrong. The second official was waving his arms as if to stop the clock, not to signal a Big Red touchdown. Joseph, he insisted, had stepped out of bounds at the Colorado 9.

The call was met with disbelief by the Husker offense, which was already leaving the field in celebration. Flummoxed at having to score two touchdowns to get 6 points, they were stuffed on third down inside the 5. Osborne went for 3, but got 0, as Gregg Barrios pulled the point-blank field-goal attempt wide.

Nebraska eventually would get the points back in the third quarter, on a 46-yard bomb from Joseph to freshman tight end Johnny Mitchell that pushed the lead to 12-0. The ensuing two-point conversion failed, but none of us really cared. The public-address announcer had just informed us Georgia Tech had knocked off top-ranked Virginia on a last-second field goal. Somewhere in the dryness of the press box, Devaney was watching as his master stroke began to take form.

And then the fourth quarter arrived.

It was just a simple isolation play, and that's what made it so difficult to watch as Nebraska failed and failed and failed again to stop it. Hagan would turn and hand the ball off to his tailback, Eric Bienemy, who then followed his fullback through the hole and past a tied-up linebacker. Colorado must have run that play two dozen times in the final quarter, in which they rallied for 27 straight points to bury the Cornhuskers. NU tried gamely to respond in the closing minutes, but staring into a nasty, spitting wind and the onrushing Buffaloes, the Cornhuskers iced over. Game, set, match, and league title to Colorado.

In trying to swallow the bitter failure, I had decided the contest had turned on just a handful of plays: Mickey Joseph's alleged out-of-bounds run; CU's recovery of its own fumble at the Nebraska 2 while still trailing 12-7; Osborne's unsuccessful fake-punt call with six minutes left that, for all intents and purposes, had sealed the Huskers' fate. Maybe, I thought as I splashed through icy puddles along Fourteenth Street on my way to my car, the Cornhuskers still had an outside shot at playing for the national title. But in my heart of hearts I knew there was no debating it. Yet another autumn of promise had given way to the harsh realities of November.

An argument can be made that the 1990 team was one bad quarter removed from playing for the title in the Orange Bowl. But in actuality, it wasn't even close. Following a downcast victory in Lawrence, Kansas, the next week, the Cornhuskers went to Norman and got steamrolled by a three-loss Oklahoma Sooner squad and topped it off by mailing in a 24-point loss to Georgia Tech in the Florida Citrus Bowl.

The Big Red played in that final game, but they really didn't. By the time they took the field against the Yellow Jackets, the Huskers looked like a bad photocopy of the team that I'd seen play earlier in the year. When the final Associated Press poll came out on January 2, the Big Red had slouched all the way to twenty-fourth, twenty-three whole spots behind the national champion Buffaloes. Things were a bit better in the coaches' poll – NU was seventeenth. But the unforgiving truth was this: The 1990 squad was one of Tom Osborne's worst, and no amount of politicking could put a good spin on that.

Mad Mike and the Hopping Cop

NEBRASKA 71, COLORADO STATE 14 – SEPTEMBER 14, 1991

There's a little drive-through Mexican place on West O Street called D'Leon's that serves tortillas as addictive as nicotine. The narrow building is painted red, white, and green, and as you pull up to the drive-through window you can't help but notice it's adorned with a picture of the Lady of Guadalupe, right next to an advertisement for international telephone calling cards. Through the window you can hear Spanish banter, and once in a while you'll see an employee sporting the ball cap of his favorite Mexican fútbol club. D'Leon's isn't much to look at, really. It's pretty much a little hole in the wall and looks like it was probably once a gas station or something, but hungry people in search of authenticity line up there, drawn like moths to a flame by the magic that goes on inside those walls.

I think of D'Leon's as the Memorial Stadium of Mexican food. Back in the '80s, *Sports Illustrated* dubbed the home of the Huskers the worst place to watch the best college football. Who could argue with that? Memorial Stadium was – is – this cruddy old stone edifice that is sort of a Frankenstein of a stadium. The designs of the end zone seats don't match those of the sidelines, the sidelines don't match each other, and the new skyboxes don't match . . . well, anything. There are some seats in the east stands from which you can see only about 80 percent of the field. And it's cramped and impossible to get around in on game days. But for a few golden hours each weekend, no one really cares. There's lots of magic that goes on inside *those* walls too.

Before '94 a big part of Football Saturday's allure and charm came from the crowd. With the suspense usually gone from the actual football game by halftime, you couldn't help but be drawn in by the rhythm and tempo of the red-clad horde, with its chants and its cheers and, most of all, its odd and memorable characters. About the

59

time the band would pump out "Glory of the Gridiron" during the pregame show, you could count on the sight of "Husker" Bob Rowe, covered in red and white, waving signs at the crowd and making his Big Red Womp-It puppet punch the air. By the time I'd started regularly attending games, the origin of Memorial Stadium's self-anointed cheerleader had become the stuff of legend. As the story goes, Husker Bob got his start in the south stands in 1978. Tired of the fans around him being so negative, he tossed his Irish-style touring cap down over the fence, climbed down to get it, waited until the game action moved to the north side of the field, and then cut straight across the Astroturf over to where the band was sitting. You'd think that stadium officials would have knocked Bob on his keister, but then again, Husker Bob was fully clothed and did not appear to have any long hair. By the fourth game of that season, the band got permission for him to hang out with them. He spent the next thirteen years roving along the front-row walkway of the stadium, cajoling and inspiring fans.

Then there was Mad Mike, the wildman who wore a tattered No. 9 jersey and a pair of stretch shorts, roaming up and down the aisles and pounding his weathered red drum. Whenever there was a lull in the action and the crowd started going all NyQuil on the Cornhuskers, you'd hear this *boomboomboomboomboomboomboom* and a hideous primal scream. Then Mad Mike would wail out something like, "Heyyyyy, are we bad?" And the nearest section was obliged to respond, "We're baaaaaaaaad." Mike was also responsible for the very first Wave rolling through Memorial Stadium. I was at that game in 1984, when the Cornhuskers were mauling Lou Holtz's Minnesota Golden Gophers. Mad Mike stood at the base of the south stands like a conductor, first directing one section to stand and then turning to the next section over and ordering, "Now, over here!" And before long, the Wave was rolling like thunder around the old ballpark. About the only guy who wasn't amused was Tom Osborne, one eye squinting into the sun as he looked around the stands in disbelief. I guess I can't blame him – Mad Mike had started the Wave when the Huskers had the ball, after all; the racket caused an illegal-procedure penalty against NU.

Across the field and along the west sideline stood Steve Potter, a bearded and long-haired lawyer from Gothenburg who dressed in a vested suit with three-quarter length sleeves and high-water pants, knee-high socks, and saddle shoes. He would spend Football Saturday winging foil-wrapped hot dogs to anyone within throwing range. On a still day, that meant anyone sitting below the fortieth row or so. The guy was deadly accurate and could even fling wieners behind his back. The recipient of the hot dog would unwrap it, stuff his payment in the foil and fling it back down toward Potter, and everyone would dutifully applaud. Potter was so popular that other concessionaires tried to mimic him – for instance, a dude who resembled a chubby Michael Keaton who wore a referee's shirt chucked hot dogs into the crowd along the east sideline too. But he wasn't as good as Steve, particularly when it came to specialty shots.

Heck, interacting with the vendors could have been a full-time activity. There was a rotund 7UP man who looked like Cooter from *The Dukes of Hazzard* who would make his way through the student section, round about the third quarter. In hawking his wares, he'd belt out a drawling, drawn-out "Seeeehhhvvvvvvv'n-UP!" – a call the entire section would repeat, perfectly imitating his pronunciation, intonation, and pitch. He was one of the most popular pop sellers in the whole house, but I don't really know whether he ever made a sale.

By the end of the third quarter, you'd turn toward the southeast corner, where the stadium's foundation jutted into the sky like a giant set of steps. Each step was about five feet high, and that became the stage for the Hopping Cop. You could set your watch to when this member of Lincoln's Finest would begin his ascent, rapidly swinging his leg onto the top of the next step and then pulling his body up. He wouldn't stop until he got all the way to the top of the stadium. It was like watching that "Cliffhanger" game on *The Price Is Right*, only without the yodeling. Instead, everyone would yell, "Whoa!" as he climbed another step. When he reached the top, he'd raise his hands above his head and do a little Rocky Balboa dance, and we'd all cheer his effort before turning back to the action on the field, where the fourth-stringers were dutifully mopping up a 59-7 victory over Pukestain Tech. Or in this case, 71-14 over Colorado State.

But many of the unique creatures of Memorial Stadium had already started to fade away. Just a week earlier, Husker Bob had suffered a fatal heart attack during the stormy home opener against Utah State, a fate Husker fans reflected upon with both sadness and envy: It was tragic that Husker Bob had left this earth, but hey, if you're gonna buy it, what better place to do it than Memorial Stadium? By this point it was getting difficult to find the hot dog–throwing lawyer and his east stands counterpart too. And, of course, Mad Mike had already taken his act to the University of Kansas a few years earlier in search of a paycheck. Only the Hopping Cop remained, really. Sadly, his days were also limited. In just three years, the placement of a HuskerVision screen in the stadium's southeast corner would eliminate the space he required to make his leaps up the stone steps. It was only the second game of the 1991 season when Nebraska pounded on the Rams, but the undercurrent at the stadium that day was one of finality, as if an era that we didn't even know had fully existed was now passing.

These days the game is played before a live studio audience. The packaging of the spectacle, it seems, is just as important as the game on the field. Football Saturday is more meticulously choreographed than a Madonna concert, and that leaves no room for spontaneity. Husker Bob's Big Red Womp-It could never hope to compete with the mesmerizing glow of HuskerVision. A man with a hand-held drum wouldn't stand a chance against the booming stereo speakers throughout the stadium blaring such timeless and inspiring anthems as "Kickstart My Heart." So we sit, silent and awestruck by the omnipresent video screens, mostly because the public address announcer tells us to. The "alternative" cheerleading is now done by a university-sponsored dance team dressed in sequined red leotards. Down on the sidelines hot dogs still take flight into the crowd, but the man behind the antics isn't an oddball vendor looking to clear fifty dollars for the day, or maybe even seventy-five if he really hustles. He's an officially licensed corporate partner who uses an air-powered, hot dog–shaped gun to blast wienies up into the nosebleed sections. Somewhere, Steve Potter must be grimacing.

I understand that many of the changes in Memorial Stadium have upgraded the fan experience. Yes, it's pleasant to plant one's gluteus maximus on Fiberglas seats instead of on ones made of rotting, gray wood. Yes, it's helpful when the public address system doesn't cut out every five minutes. And yes, the instant replay screens have enhanced fans' access to the on-field happenings, both for the people who need it (the people who sit in front of the end zone stands and watch through a chain-link fence) and for the people who just think they need it (the indignant cranks who claim to spot a holding call against the Huskers' opponent on every single replay). And I'm sure it's more profitable for the athletic department to show commercials on HuskerVision during timeouts than it is to let the band play the school song. But there's nothing real about it anymore, nothing genuine. This is nowhere more clearly illustrated than by how the crowd interacts with the game. We used to be part of it, but now we're just another prop in the production. The machines tell us when to cheer, where to watch, and what clothes to wear. Somewhere on the way to the bank, the athletic department turned game day into a game show.

As I found my seat at a recent game, I saw a guy off to my right who had brought along his nine-year-old son. This was the little guy's first Memorial Stadium experience, the man said excitedly, as if this was a day he'd been waiting to share with his son his whole life. Sometime during the second quarter, I happened to glance over and see the man intently watching the action on the field, but his son was craning his neck up at HuskerVision. A little bit later, I looked over again. The little dude was still staring at the big TV – not just between plays, the whole damn time. As far as I could tell, the kid didn't once turn and watch the actual action on the field. His father, in essence, paid fifty bucks for his son to watch the entire thing on television.

When the game ended, the boy's father asked him what his favorite part of the evening had been. The boy stopped for a minute to think, presumably going over the myriad sights and sounds the venerable old stadium had offered up that evening. But do you know what the kid's answer was? The Amigo's "shell game" contest on the HuskerVision screens. Yeah, the video game with three Cornhusker helmets, and one of them has the Amigo's emblem under it, and you have to guess which one it is after the computer shuffles them all around. That was what this child had taken away from the whole experience: an ad for a Mexican fast-food chain.

Needless to say, the dad looked disappointed. He took his boy by the hand, and together they started down the north stadium steps. As they reached the tunnel, the boy turned to his dad and asked, "Can we stop at Amigo's on the way home?"

Fine by me, kid, I thought. That's one less car in line at D'Leon's.

Culture Club

There's an old saying football coaches tell players to convey their distaste for celebrations after touchdowns. It goes, "Son, if you make it to the end zone, try to act like you've been there before."

Most Nebraskans agree with that axiom, along with the other hallowed pillars of the Cornhusker Way: Win with class, lose with dignity, respect your opponent, and for the love of Christ, wear red pants when you're playing on the road.

Before the 1992 season, however, the Cornhusker team leadership broke with that last tradition. They voted to wear white bottoms, not red ones, during away games. This transformed NU's once-slick road outfits into something vaguely resembling a set of tennis whites. Needless to say, the move was met with massive disapproval by us Nebraskans. Uniform gimmickry wasn't cool. Such tactics were for the Okie States and Missouris of the world to rally around when they couldn't find anything real to motivate them – say, contending for a spot in the top half of the conference standings. Just suiting up for Nebraska should have been enough motivation to win.

The players were dumbfounded as to why everyone was so upset. Well, the tradition obviously meant more to us than it did to them. And because they would be gone from the program in just a few years (and we'd still be here), we felt like someone should have checked with us.

That sentiment grew after NU lost its first road game of the year – to the second-ranked Washington Huskies in Seattle – while wearing the surrenderlike disaster suits. I watched that loss from a sports bar on my girlfriend's twenty-first birthday, while over in the corner a couple of drunk Husker fans sat and commiserated. A red-clad woman complained how awful the team looked in its new getup; the bearded man next to her lamented what was shaping up to be the Cornhuskers' eighth straight loss to a ranked foe. To him the 29-14 setback symbolized more than the demise of NU's good fashion sense. The loss to the Huskies signaled the death throes of another, much more important tradition: winning.

64

"We're gonna start missing out on the good recruits if we don't turn things around quick," he moaned. "There ain't a black kid in the country who would want to come freeze their ass off in Lincoln if they can't play for a winner." Translation: The absence of color – whether it's on the uniform or the roster – makes the Cornhuskers bad.

The woman sat silently for a few seconds, watching as Mike Grant threw an incompletion. She took a swig of beer. "Yeah," she replied. "And then they'll *never* be on TV."

And that, I suspect, would have been the end of this particular couple's exposure to black people. In the lives of many Nebraskans, African Americans only exist on television. This is the sad result of Plains demographics – that is, there are basically no black people here. Barely 2 percent of Nebraska's population is of African descent, and that number is more or less huddled in the state's two metropolitan centers. Even there, in our enlightened urban capitals, old stereotypes and prejudices persist and segregate the black and white communities, at least socially. When out-of-staters liken a trip through Nebraska as warping back to the 1950s, they're not just talking about the rural quaintness of the place.

Unfortunately, lots of Nebraskans are forced to look at race relations from a theoretical viewpoint. Because TV is our main source of information on people of color, many of us hold the common misconception that all black men are either athletes, entertainers, or criminals. We also don't understand why BET is on the basic cable lineup and the Golf Channel is on the digital tier. But we fully understand the need to recruit speed – that's a sports euphemism for "black kids" – so Dear Old Nebraska U. can stay among the nation's elite football programs. So we let it slide.

Five minutes after stepping foot on campus, I was starkly aware of the fact I was no longer in Rosalie. And by the time I reached my senior year, I'd made acquaintances with a number of black students. Though looking back, those I met invariably were athletes. In Harper Hall I lived next door to Clifford Scales, the starting point guard for the basketball team, and through him I met a number of hoops players. A few years later I became acquainted with Calvin Jones, a prodigious I-back for Tom Osborne's football team. Well, I sat next to Calvin in history class, anyway. He knew me by my first name and we'd often nod to each other and say "S'up" if we ever crossed paths at the Nebraska Union.

Mostly our conversations before history classes were quick and I imagine would have been pretty funny to an outside observer. I tried to sound a little bit black and Calvin tried to sound a little bit white. I dragged out words, lowered my voice about a half-octave, and added slight emphasis on certain vowels. As for Calvin, it was clear he spoke differently to me than he did to his black friends. To his immediate right sat defensive end Donta Jones, and when the two of them interacted, it was like listening to an entirely different language. So I got the sense I was never able to meet the *real* Calvin Jones, just the version he figured I wanted to see.

The University of Nebraska–Lincoln is probably the most diverse area in the entire state. But in many ways it's exactly like the rest of Nebraska. For one, the student body is 95 percent white. Meanwhile, most of the big-sport athletes are black. Therefore they're some of the school's highest-profile students, especially when Brad Nessler and Gary Danielson are in town doing the ABC Game of the Week. But they're virtually invisible the rest of the time. Oh, back then you would see them once in a while, walking in small bands along our broad, white sidewalks. You'd spot them in class, grouped together in the back of the classroom and being largely ignored (or singled out) by the professor. But what you rarely saw anywhere was them mixing with white students. For one reason or another, each group kept its distance from the other. Yet, on Saturdays at Memorial Stadium, thousands of white students yelled in support of their exploits. We called them by their first names as if they were old friends. We referred to them as "we" and "us."

About that time, a popular T-shirt worn by African American students used to read: "It's a Black Thang That You Wouldn't Understand." Fair enough. But just from watching, I did make a few observations. The culture of the black athlete was striking amid our homogeny. They were more expressive, more lively, more intense, and more assertive. We often ignored our impulses and downplayed our feelings. They often reveled in them.

I caught a flash of this, and another side of Calvin Jones, on Halloween 1992, the day Nebraska hosted Colorado in the de facto Big 8 championship game. But that sighting was from my spot in Memorial Stadium, not the seat I once had next to him in history. NU and CU were each rated eighth by the Associated Press, and the Buffs were riding a twenty-five-game unbeaten streak in Big 8 play.

Though the Cornhuskers hadn't beaten Colorado since 1988, there was cause for hope this year. One week earlier, the latest in a long line of Next Turner Gills – a freshman from Bradenton, Florida, named Tommie Frazier – led the Cornhuskers to a road win over Missouri. Frazier had that unmistakable coolness about him that calmed the most high-strung fan, and that his first home start came against the Huskers' despised rival seemed to be a good omen: Gill's home debut as NU's starter came against the same Buffaloes eleven years earlier.

It was one of those charmed afternoons where everything went right, and the complexion of the game was a perfect script for a young quarterback like Frazier to gain confidence for the season's stretch run. On the first play, Travis Hill intercepted a Koy Detmer pass, and moments later Calvin went in for a touchdown. Then, early in the second quarter, Tyrone Hughes returned a Buff punt to the CU 47, setting NU up with a short field. You could sense something big was about to happen.

On the first play following the return, Frazier wheeled and handed the ball to Calvin, who hit the right side of the Buffalo line at full speed. Rob Zatechka and Will Shields caved in a pair of Colorado defenders, and diminutive wideout Abdul Muhammad took out the final Buffalo in No. 44's path to the end zone. The rest was history. As the referee flung up his hands to signal 6 points and Memorial Stadium exploded into a torrent of white noise, Calvin threw the ball down, ripped off his helmet, and released a triumphant yell up toward the stands. It made the hairs on my arms stand at attention.

Calvin's emphatic touchdown blast was emblematic of how everyone in Memorial Stadium felt that day. Before long, it was 24-7, then 38-7, and finally 52-7. When this dominating, richly satisfying victory was finally over, my old history buddy had racked up three touchdowns and led all rushers. I couldn't help but appreciate the triumph a little bit more because I "knew" Calvin, and it was gratifying to see when he got to the end zone, he ignored the old maxim and acted like he'd never been there before.

Two weeks later, the Cornhuskers put on their road whites again and promptly got schooled by miserable Iowa State in Ames. After the shocking loss – the only defeat Osborne would suffer to a squad that finished with a losing record – the team ditched the all-white motif and donned the traditional red pants for the next road game, against Oklahoma. The Huskers went on to pound OU 33-9.

The following week I saw Calvin walking on campus amid a group of about a half-dozen other black students. I didn't talk to him. It seemed at the time that our best connection was as player and fan, not as friends or even random schoolmates. He had the pads off, I had put my red away for another week, and we were back in our separate worlds. Those places just happened to exist on top of one another.

Worn Down

NEBRASKA 27, OKLAHOMA STATE 13 - OCTOBER 7, 1993

By the time I'd reached my fifth and final year at the university, I'd decided the members of the Nebraska football team were sort of like cigarette smoke, ultraviolet rays, and Billy Ray Cyrus: The less you were exposed to them, the better off you were.

I didn't get season tickets that fall. Aside from the annual season-ending conflagration against Oklahoma, the '93 home schedule had more dogs than the local animal shelter. The highlight of the non-conference campaign was when some spot on the map called North Texas came to Lincoln. The bigger reason, though, was that in my years at UNL I'd adopted a measure of disdain for the culture of football, which I thought occupied a disproportionate amount of the local zeitgeist. I felt no need to donate any more time or money to a cause I supported less with each passing day, and resolved to buy single-game tickets if I suddenly regressed and needed a football fix. I was scheduled to graduate in May, and my course load was piled sky-high; Saturdays could be used for (gasp) studying.

There were other reasons football became more distant. Between seeing players nearly running down pedestrians while at the wheel of their new BMWs and hearing about them grabbing women's crotches at downtown bars, I'd grown weary of their off-field antics. For the past several years I'd worked for the *Daily Nebraskan*, the student-run campus newspaper, which had chronicled many of their extra-curricular activities. There were a few stories that never saw print, of course. Let's just say the image created by the South Stadium spin machine and the one I had formed based on real-life experiences were on two different ends of the public-relations spectrum.

It was ironic. One reason I chose UNL was because it was the scar-let-and-cream home of the Huskers (a nifty bonus was that it was also the scarlet-and-cream home of a top-notch journalism school). I had settled on the university when I was nine, when my brave Big Red champions towered over my fourth-grade imagination like an army of colossuses. But now I'd gotten too close to the object of my obsession, and those mythical boyhood images had been shattered. Familiarity had bred contempt – well, familiarity and a clinical case of Generation X cynicism, anyway. On top of that, I was training to be a journalist, a job that pays you to be skeptical. I didn't have to search long for a machine to rage against.

It's doubtful I was the first Husker fanboy to sour on his heroes. The football culture on campus has been so universal, so pervasive, so damn huge for so long, it most certainly has created nearly as many nonconformists as it has wild-eyed groupies. The Cornhuskers were the closest thing we had to celebrities, after all. And like most celebrities, they were best viewed from afar. Otherwise, like me, you ran the risk of seeing them for who they really were, and that ruined the whole fantasy.

Compounding the matter was that through four games, the 1993 team was playing a listless, one-dimensional brand of football. They were unbeaten, but Tom Osborne was still sledgehammering away at defenses with the run, safe in the adage of wearing the other team down. Week after week this was the strategy: Line up, snap ball, ram down opponent's cakehole, repeat as necessary.

It looked positively Neolithic, especially compared to the high-tech attacks being run in places like Tallahassee, Gainesville, and Miami. The play calling was in part dictated by early injuries to quarterback Tommie Frazier and I-back Calvin Jones, which had turned a Husker offense that was expected to be a bitchin' Camaro into an Olds Delta 88 with a bad fuel pump. It was as ugly as it was predictable – but effective.

Nebraska's first league foe of the '93 campaign was Oklahoma State, an average bunch whose defense was tougher than the cardboard cutouts they usually propped up to stop other teams. Osborne, who was sitting at 199 wins, would go for a coaching milestone in Stillwater on a Thursday night in front of an espn audience.

As my roommates Rob and Gerry plopped onto our sofa and tuned in, I retreated to my room. I had an art history test the next day and had decided in a moment of staggering maturity to study instead. While noble, this was as fruitless as a Midwestern barbecue. I attempted to concentrate on the difference between Manet and Monet for a while, but with each minute it got harder. I could hear Rob and Gerry reacting to nearly every play, and from the sound of it they weren't very pleased. It was quite possible the Huskers needed me.

So I came out of my room. Gerry and Rob had the TV sound turned down and KFAB's Kent Pavelka, who was noting Nebraska was trailing the Cowboys at halftime, turned up. Apparently NU had tried the whole irresistible-force-meets-immovable-object approach and had been repeatedly stuffed. Someone had forgotten to tell Osborne that all four of Okie State's team captains were starting defensive linemen. It wasn't until Frazier was forced to the air in the final minutes of the half that the Cornhuskers moved the ball.

I hunkered down on the couch. Rob slid over and said Osborne would have to start throwing in the second half. But instead of flinging the ball around, Nebraska started running wide, using Frazier's speed and elusiveness to bust some plays. Lo and behold, it began to work. When No. 15 slipped into the end zone from 4 yards out, it capped a seven-play, 56-yard touchdown drive, almost all of which had been on the ground. You could see the tide start to turn: The hairline fractures in the Okie State defense were becoming cracks. Then holes. Then gaping chasms. If you didn't know better, you could almost detect a smile on Dr. Tom's face. The relentless pounding was taking its toll.

Early in the fourth quarter, linebacker Trev Alberts sacked Cowboy quarterback Toné Jones for an enormous loss to force OSU to punt from its own 3. And on the next play, magic happened. Cornerback Barron Miles came off the edge, rushed in at Oklahoma State's punter, flew into the air, and blocked the kick. Rob, Gerry, and I searched the screen frantically for the football – it had to be bounding around somewhere in the Cowboy end zone – but the cameras never left Miles, who had fallen right onto the pigskin to record the unassisted double play. Touchdown, Nebraska. It was one of the most fearless feats of athleticism I'd ever seen; even the slow-motion replays couldn't do it justice. Miles got up, showed the official the ball, and was promptly mobbed by his teammates. We were dumbstruck. So was Cowboy coach Pat Jones, as ESPN cut to a shot of him. His pained expression told the story. There was no escape.

For me, either. Just like the Cornhuskers' relentless running attack, my affection for the Big Red kept chipping away at my layers of cynicism, pounding and pounding until I finally gave in. Sure, I thought as Calvin Jones ripped off a long touchdown sprint, some of these guys probably weren't the most likable people on the planet. Well, neither was Woody Allen after we learned he was secretly nailing his stepdaughter, but that didn't make *Annie Hall* any less brilliant.

My friend Beau used to say it best: "The Huskers are like my family. I don't love 'em because they're good, I love 'em because they're *mine.*" Over the years, whenever I've felt the itch to sever my cerebral ties with the Big Red, I always come back to that statement and reflect upon those powerful ties that bind. The Cornhuskers are, in a way, my family. They can be exhausting and infuriating and annoying and embarrassing. Sometimes I try to disown them, and I denounce my own name. But then in the blink of an eye, a 5-foot-8 cornerback literally steals the football off the opposing punter's foot, and all is forgiven.

Two Loves

NEBRASKA 21, OKLAHOMA 7 – NOVEMBER 26, 1993

Here are two things to remember as you go through life: 1) Don't believe everything you see on ESPN; and 2) The love of a good woman is priceless, even if she doesn't know the difference between sprint options and stock options.

I'll tackle that first one first. As the 1993 season chugged on, Nebraska continued to win and climb the charts. NU prevailed in a shootout over Kansas State, put the usual drubbing on Ole Mizzou at home, and then went to Boulder to play the hated Colorado Buffaloes. In that match, which determined the inside track to the Orange Bowl, NU raced to a 21-3 lead and then hung on for a thrilling 4-point win. Victory wasn't assured until late in the game, when John Reece intercepted a Kordell Stewart pass to send CU fans cursing into the streets, searching for things to pilfer or maim or light on fire, as is their custom after they lose a game. Or after they win a game, come to think of it.

To make things even more interesting, the unbeaten Cornhuskers ascended to No. 1 in the coaches' poll in mid-November. This was pretty exciting for us Husker fans – during my college years we'd grown accustomed to the low-rent district of the national polls – but apparently ours were the only fancies being tickled. Around the country, NU was still widely perceived as a paper tiger that promptly got stuffed when it ran up against Southern schools.

A lot of this sentiment was generated by ESPN analyst Craig James. Week after week, James assailed NU during the network's broadcasts, ticking off a familiar list of grievances: *The Huskers' record has been propped up against weak opponents . . . their offense is one-dimensional . . . they've been downright lucky to get a couple of their wins . . . and please, let's not forget, this is the same crew who has lost six straight bowl games.* By the time Oklahoma Week arrived, James was more hated here than Barry Switzer, Howard Schnellenberger, and Bill McCartney combined.

All of which is part of the modern-day college football spectacle, I suppose. Every sports network sits three or four guys at a desk and has them bark about the day's action, offer some conjecture about next week's games, and argue over who should play in the title game. Usually they're doing that last one by late August. This is all done to create storylines, which in turn boosts ratings.

To make it work, each person at the desk has a part to play. One guy's the hero; one guy's the villain. One will be a sappy underdog lover; another will be a stuffy traditionalist. One will seem level-headed; another will look like a regionally biased blowhard. And true to form, one will become the designated Husker-hater for the year. Who knows what they really think. That's why you shouldn't believe everything you see on ESPN.

Though artificial, the televised college football pundits wield enormous influence on the rankings. They shape perception, perception shapes the polls, and the polls shape the championship picture. This was a problem in Nebraska during the 1993 stretch run. NU was among four teams in the national debate over who was No. 1, and it was possible the title chase could be twisted by a few choice words from someone with as small a brain as Craig James's.

I'll admit it: I raged at James along with everyone else. For the first time in awhile, the Huskers were a big part of my life; I had put them at arm's length for much of the early '90s to make room for Incredibly Mature College Things, but now they were back. As it happened, my so-so feelings toward the Cornhuskers had less to do with R.E.M., Raymond Carver, or live music at Duffy's Tavern than it did with Charlie McBride's slow-footed linebackers getting beat to

the corner. Strangely enough when the Huskers began stifling opponents with their 4-3 defensive sets and climbing to the top of the
coaches' poll, my affection for them returned. So it was no problem
to put aside *Automatic for the People* and *M is for Millions* and "What
We Talk About When We Talk About Love," so I could put more focus
on my first love.

What I hadn't banked on, however, was that by then I'd have *another* love.

Kathy and I had been together for nearly two years. We met in a
class, were good friends for a while, developed crushes on each other,
then finally quit trying to fool ourselves. Over the next two years, we
became about as close as two people could be.

Well, aside from my whole attempt to mask how much of a full-
blown Husker freak I was, that is. I had dropped hints from time to
time, but she'd never really shown any interest in the team. Besides,
in the crowd we ran with – that ironic literary hipster crowd that
exists at every university – Husker worship was treated as a character
flaw. And this was ok; before I'd met Kathy, I'd often treated the days
between football games as so much filler time, but now I'd found a
life – a real life, not the kind whose highs and lows were dictated by
how well the team performed on Saturday. It was nice, and I didn't
want to mess up a good thing.

It was easy to rein in my passion in the humdrum Keithen Mc-
Cant/Mike Grant era. But now that Tommie Frazier and the Huskers
had made the long climb back to the top, there was no way I could
contain my enthusiasm. So during Oklahoma Week, I started trolling
for tickets.

The only hope I had was a "maybe" from one of my journalism
professors, who planned to see how cold it would be on game day
before deciding if he would go. On the morning of the game, he
called to say it was too damn cold and he was too damn old. His two
tickets were mine.

Hot damn. I spent the next forty-five minutes on the phone trying to coax someone to go with me: Gerry. Rob. Todd. Chuck. Blake.
Kevin. Jason. Matt. Mike. Brent. Andy. Mark. Anthony. No takers, not
one, for a primo ticket to the game of the year. Either they were still
gone for Thanksgiving or they had retained their senses and planned
to watch the game from the warmth of their living rooms.

I looked at my watch. It was three hours until kickoff. I didn't want to take a bath on the second ticket, and I sure as hell didn't want to go to the big game by myself. Who could I get on such short notice?

As if on cue, Kathy came out of the bedroom, rubbing sleep from her eyes.

And this is how, two and a half hours later, on the coldest and snowiest day of 1993, we found ourselves sitting in wet, borrowed seats in the east stadium. I was there to watch Nebraska go for an unbeaten year and the right to play for the national championship. Kathy was there because she agreed to come along on my promise that if the game was basically decided by halftime, we'd leave and never speak of it again. While I was glued to the action, she shivered, hugged herself for warmth, and stared blankly at the back of the head of the person in front of her.

As if to spite her, the Sooners marched 74 yards for a touchdown. It was looking worse early in the second quarter, when Jerald Moore zipped past the first line of Blackshirts and took off on one of those see-ya-later runs that we Cornhusker fans are so used to seeing from Oklahoma running backs. But before my ice-addled brain could think, "Oh, no, 14-0," Moore was tackled from behind around the Husker 15 and lost the football. From out of nowhere, NU's Donta Jones scooped up the ball and saved the day.

Nebraska eventually got across the goal line – a short Frazier run following a Sooner turnover – and the old rivals went to the locker rooms tied. Kathy looked at me hopefully. No dice.

As the game wore on, the two teams seemed determined to play to a stalemate. It wasn't until early in the fourth quarter that Nebraska's offense woke up. After getting a short field to work with, Frazier drove NU to the Oklahoma 11, where it was third and nine. No. 15 retreated to the pocket, then zipped a pass to Abdul Muhammad, who twisted his way into the end zone. Finally, the Huskers had broken through. With as much relief as euphoria, Memorial Stadium rumbled with the dull *thud thud thud* of gloved hands.

On the ensuing kickoff, the Sooners' Darrius Johnson was stripped of the ball, and No. 22, David Seizys, pounced on it at the OU 20. One play later, Calvin Jones sprinted around left side, shrugged off a tackler, and crashed into the end zone. With two touchdowns in thirteen seconds, NU had seized control.

Sensing history was about to be made, the whole stadium shrugged off subzero wind chills and rose, guiding the Blackshirts home as they turned Oklahoma away time and again. As the clock ran out, fans poured onto the Astroturf, wrapping themselves around the goalposts. In mere moments, the joyous mass brought the posts crashing down, dismantled them, and sped them on their way downtown, as was tradition. The Huskers had done it – 11-0. They were unbeaten. They were headed to the Orange Bowl. They were going to go down there and get Dr. Tom his first title.

The whole ride back to Kathy's apartment, I chattered away about what I had just seen – Frazier's bullet pass and Muhammad's score and the bam-bam touchdowns that pushed the charmed Huskers into the title game. She let me rave for a while, then asked if I wanted to see a movie. A movie. Here Kathy had just borne witness to one of the single biggest triumphs in the history of the school, one of the greatest days in Nebraska since January 1, 1972, and she had basically said, "That was nice. Want to go see *Jurassic Park* at the Starship 9?" The writing on the wall was clear: We wouldn't be going to a Husker game together any time soon.

This was very disappointing at the time. But over the years, I've come to learn that loving her as well as the Huskers – and keeping them in two very separate worlds – is good for me. Once a week, I bid her farewell for a few hours as I retreat to my he-man clubhouse, dressed in my ceremonial battle garb. She reads a book, goes shopping, or rides her bike, oblivious to the righteous crusade about to take place down on campus. When I come home, she listens patiently to my expert recap of the Big Red's latest performance, eventually finds an opening in my monologue, and then pulls me back into the real world.

I know it can't be easy, especially during the season. She tolerates my Cornhusker-induced pouts. She puts up with my mood swings and touchiness before, during, and after televised games. She allows me to explain football minutiae to her as she passes by on her way upstairs. Her patience has been undoubtedly tried by my constant intensity for the team, and Lord knows how much explaining she's had to do for me when she goes alone to family gatherings that had the nerve to take place on Football Saturdays.

Often, I think, it must baffle her to see the man she knows so well turn into an unrecognizable moron whenever red jerseys and white helmets are involved. But maybe she's not baffled at all. She gets me just fine. She may not know why I'm the way I am, but she understands *how* I am. She grasps precisely how important Nebraska football is to me and sees the happiness it can bring me and doesn't try to question or change that. She tries to share in it, though deep down I know she couldn't care less.

In other words, she likes me for me, scarlet baggage and all. Whenever I have doubts about that, I think back to that dreadful November day and the image of her sitting there, freezing and miserable, just for a chance to see me at my most happy.

Prejudice and Pride

FLORIDA STATE 18, NEBRASKA 16 - JANUARY 1, 1994

To be a Nebraskan is to live with the knowledge that sometimes the other school's goalposts have to fall. In forty years of dominating college football, we've accepted the role of Philistine, constantly staving off upset bids and enduring every motivational gimmick our opponent can dream up: the hey-let's-wear-pants-the-same-color-as-our-jerseys ploy; the triple-double-reverse-handoff-pitch-pass to the left offensive tackle; the other team entering the field through the student section to the pounding of Samoan war drums. We've seen it all.

Sixty minutes of play and 500 yards of offense later, the Huskers usually make all the shenanigans look silly. But once in a while, when the planets are aligned just right or if Delmar in Broken Bow doesn't say his prayers properly, Nebraska will lose one it shouldn't, and the goal posts in places like Stillwater or Ames make an unfortunate trip to the turf. As painful as this is, I suppose it's also sort of a compliment. A win versus Nebraska means something. No one tears down the goalposts after a win versus, say, Utah State.

This is how it was in the early '90s, at least in a regional sense. In the Midwest, the Huskers were still the biggest dog on the porch, and a victory over them was a *cause célèbre* – even if it wasn't that way anywhere else. Nationally, NU was seriously short on street cred. All the Big 8 titles in the world couldn't mask the perception Nebraska was nothing more than a regional bully. The Huskers had lost six straight bowl games, and lost them badly; the hulking linemen who pushed Kansas around in October looked plodding in January, powerless to deal with college football's latest death squads, Florida State and Miami.

Our common response was that Nebraska wasn't as bad as it looked, the other teams were just that good: From the 1988 Fiesta Bowl to the 1993 Orange Bowl, Nebraska's bowl opponents finished second, second, third, first, first, and second nationally. While this got us through the winter OK, we were still unsettled. With every New Year's loss, 1971 became more and more distant, our system was looking more suited for a museum, and the cries for change got louder.

Me, I'd gotten the sense that I'd come along about ten years too late to truly enjoy Husker football. For years only Oklahoma had stood between us and a national championship. When we finally beat OU on a regular basis, Colorado rose up to crush our dreams. Dr. Tom eventually solved the Buffs but then found the way completely impassable by the ultimate foes – Florida schools that were swift, nasty, and completely unbending.

By New Year's Day 1994, I'd accumulated a healthy dislike for the Florida State Seminoles. Let me count the ways: There was their Southern-fried coach, Bobby Bowden; there was their fans' decidedly un-PC war chant and tomahawk chop, ripped off from the Atlanta Braves; there was their sweetheart status with the national media; and there was the fact they lost their biggest regular-season game to Notre Dame but still found themselves No. 1 at year's end, ahead of Nebraska and two other unbeatens in the writers' poll.

But apparently, I was in the minority. Not a question was raised around the nation when Florida State was selected to face NU in the Orange Bowl, leaving unbeaten West Virginia at No. 3 and howling about good-ol'-boy politics. It fell on deaf ears – the storyline wasn't in boring old Morgantown, it was in sunny Miami, where FSU had rolled into town on a wave of hype. Meantime, the oddsmakers tabbed FSU as 17 1/2-point favorites.

Now, we all knew that up and down the roster, Nebraska probably wasn't as talented as Florida State. We understood FSU had superhuman dual-threat quarterback and Heypesman Trophy winner Charlie Ward. And we grasped that statistically the Seminoles commanded the nation's No. 1 offense *and* defense. But, great googily-moogily, 17 1/2 *points?* Who did they think we were, Baylor? This wasn't just disrespect, this was an outrage.

But we kept it to ourselves. After getting our tambourines kicked for six Januarys in a row, we had acquired a skill for pre-bowl tongue-biting. When in doubt, shut your piehole and hope to God Almighty that your team does its talking on the field.

Hope. There's that word again. This was one of those times that illustrated the difference between hope and belief. Husker fans in the early 1990s *believed* NU would pound on Missouri but were only able to *hope* the Huskers could keep it respectable against Florida State. As the new year arrived at Duffy's Tavern, some frat boys began the drunken Go Big Red cheer (you know the one: "Gooo-oo Bii-iiig Re-edddd . . . GOBIGRED!") and I raised my bottle in their direction and joined in. Still, I thought, NU's undefeated season was probably coming to an end in just twenty-three short hours. It was sad realizing this would be the final game I'd witness as a student at the university and knowing it would probably end in another crushing loss.

What didn't occur to me was that while Bowden's megastars had been preparing for the Orange Bowl for about five weeks, Nebraska had been getting ready for this game for about five years. Shortly after FSU blasted the Huskers 41-17 in the 1990 Fiesta Bowl, Tom Osborne and his assistants shifted their recruiting focus toward speed and agility instead of size and power. The transformation was slow and subtle – not every blue-chipper wanted to leave Bradenton, Florida, to stare at piles of dirty snow in Lincoln – but it was taking shape. Where Danny Noonan once lumbered, Trev Alberts now prowled. Defensive backs became linebackers and attacked with abandon in Charlie McBride's new 4-3 scheme. The offense, while still run-oriented, had become more than the one-dimensional leviathan it was assumed to be. While the national media genuflected to FSU and I clung to desperate, drunken wishes, Dr. Tom was setting his trap.

The trap was sprung with six minutes left in the first half. Florida State was ahead 3-0, and while Nebraska was still in the game, it was tenuous at best. The Noles' velociraptors on defense made it damn near impossible to run wide, and their eight-man fronts clogged the inside. So Osborne ordered Tommie Frazier to the air. First, the sophomore lofted a toss to No. 33, Clester Johnson, over the middle for 25 yards to the Florida State 34. On the next play, lightning struck. Tommie took the snap, stutter-stepped to his right as if to run an option, slipped back a step, and launched another one toward Clester. This time, two Seminoles crunched Johnson as the ball arrived, and it fluttered end-over-end into the Miami night sky.

Out of nowhere swooped No. 7, Reggie Baul. The sophomore split end caught the deflection in full stride, turned upfield before the stunned Seminoles could react, and bolted into the end zone untouched. It was Nebraska's first lead in a bowl game since 1990. As teammates mobbed Baul and FSU's defenders trudged off the field with hands on hips, Baul raised both hands, then jogged to the sideline in a sort of dazed disbelief. It was goddamned magnificent.

As a fan, there is simply no real-life sporting equivalent to which I can compare this transcendent moment. About the closest moment I can summon is the fight scene in the first Rocky movie, when Apollo Creed dances around the Italian Stallion cracking jokes and telling sportswriters to get their cameras ready, clearly toying with his opponent. But moments later, in a flurry of fists, the underdog Balboa connects with a demolishing uppercut that staggers the champ, depositing him on the canvas. Then the camera pans back to Rocky, standing above Creed, wide-eyed and almost as stunned as his downed foe. Reggie Baul had provided Nebraska's uppercut, and we all gaped in disbelief.

Game on: Suddenly, Lorenzo Brinkley was sweeping in and tackling running backs from behind in the backfield. Alberts was flushing Ward from the pocket or sacking him. Tyrone Williams was swatting passes away. Watching them fly around the field, I wondered if NU had intercepted some kind of long-secret code only the Florida schools had access to. TV cut to a shot of Bowden, his face screwed up with worry. There was nothing better.

In the second half, Florida State grabbed the lead on a touchdown dive by William Floyd, though the Huskers and TV replays suggested he fumbled before getting into the end zone. Midway through the third quarter, Nebraska found itself down 15-7, but began to move the ball steadily. You could see it start to happen. The offensive line was beginning to blow 'em off the ball. On the first play of the fourth quarter, freshman Lawrence Phillips consummated NU's most impressive drive. He busted off the right side behind trap blocks from Rob Zatechka and Lance Lundberg to dance into the end zone from 12 yards out.

I can think of few games like this one, where every single snap had me literally on the edge of my seat, and each play seemed to be a matter of life and death. It seems unhealthy, or unnatural at the very least, for the human system to swing from one emotional extreme to the other so quickly. By the time Nebraska got the ball back, down 2 with four and a half minutes to play, I was worn out. And the biggest mood swings I've ever experienced were still to come.

First, the peak: The play developed perfectly, exploding in a kaleidoscope of scarlet. From the Florida State 40, Frazier took the snap and dashed around the right side, where a huge opening awaited. And he was off. Near the Florida State 20, a Nole defender desperately grabbed at the back of No. 15's jersey, but Frazier kept pumping, kept fighting, and eventually broke free. He was finally drug down, by his face mask, at the Seminole 9. The Seminoles held, but kicker Byron Bennett hit the go-ahead field goal with 1:16 left.

Then, the valley: Everyone knows the story. The Blackshirts, who had played like champions all evening, disappeared. A lightning-quick drive engineered by Ward, and helped by 30 yards in penalties, ended with Scott Bentley's field goal with just twenty-one seconds left. Frazier gamely got NU back in position with a long pass to Trumane Bell with just one tick on the clock, but Bennett's last-ditch field-goal try sailed well left. The final at the Orange Bowl: Florida State 18, Nebraska 16.

I sat on the couch, holding my face in my hands for what must have been an hour, replaying Bennett's final kick over and over, and running through a litany of woulda-coulda-shouldas and if-onlys. I was exhausted but perfectly awake. And I felt terrible. In fact, it was the worst I had felt in exactly ten years. That familiar ache, that same old icy-cold hole on the right side of my heart I first felt when Turner Gill's pass fell helplessly to the turf, was back. I tried to tell myself it was just a game, but I couldn't. And, I imagine, that's something people who don't follow Cornhusker football can't understand. I've tried to explain it before, to no avail. But put simply, for us, Nebraska football is not an escape, a diversion, or some kind of entertainment. It's bigger and deeper and much too profound for it to be explained away into such common little categories. Our pain when the Cornhuskers lose is very real, and this, this was the greatest pain of all.

I flipped to the news. Tom Osborne was talking about how the team played like champions. Visions of Bernie Kosar raced through my head. The comparisons would undoubtedly be made to that other epic loss soon enough. I changed the channel. An Omaha sportscaster was interviewing Corey Dixon, pads off, under the lights in an empty Orange Bowl stadium. Dixon, in so many words, said the team hadn't come all the way to Miami to hand the trophy to FSU because some supposed experts thought it would be a good idea. This was Nebraska, he said – and they had played like Nebraska.

Looking up, I found a nugget of salvation in this seventh straight bowl loss. Something important had come from this evening: Nebraska had lost this game, true enough, but it hadn't been beaten. The pollsters would anoint FSU the best in the land, and the newspaper columns would laud the Seminoles for their gutsy victory. To the victors go the spoils, after all. But in many ways it was our night too. For all of us, the game was a show of unity and defiance, a display of all things that make us Nebraska. Being a demoralized underdog is not one of those things, and after our rebirth on that New Year's night, it was something we'd never have to be again.

Away

Iowegia

My dad's reaction to the news I was moving to Iowa City after graduation was pretty much the same as mine: "Hmmm . . . Hawkeyes."

It was not only a sentiment of distaste, it was also the sum total of our combined knowledge about the whole state of Iowa. For someone who grew up in the next state over, I sure didn't know very much about our eastern neighbor. My impression of the Hawkeye State had been forged by college football and repeated trips to Sioux City. For all I knew the entire state was like Sioux City – dark and gray and full of stockyards, smelly bodies of water, and people wandering around in Iowa Hawkeye sweatshirts. But Iowa City was where the work was, and though I was entering the situation with some trepidation, I wasn't complaining.

As it turned out, Iowa City was really quite nice, a university town in the purest sense of the word. Half the town was made up of students, and everywhere you turned, you saw the school's influence. The college-town vibe was like Lincoln's; it was young and progressive and esoterically funky, and Kathy and I found the place pretty easy to navigate. Soon we learned there was an Iowa City equivalent for all of our old haunts in Lincoln: The Lincoln hippie bar, O'Rourkes, was the Deadwood in Iowa City, while the closest doppelganger to Duffy's Tavern was a downtown dump called Joe's Place. Ted & Wally's Ice Cream was now Heyn's, and the wide-screen TVs and burgers at Brewsky's gave way to fare at the Sports Column. On the surface, the only real difference in the two towns appeared to be that the Hy-Vees in Iowa City were smaller, which meant they sometimes didn't have the brand of razor I liked. That was about it.

Well, OK, there was that whole Hawkeye thing. And from that standpoint, I had a bit of internal reconciling to do. I hadn't much cared for the Iowa Hawkeyes since I was ten, when they upset my beloved Cornhuskers in a Kinnick Stadium stunner. That started it; growing up in the over-Hawkeyed Sioux City TV market and having to endure anti-Husker screeds from the odious western Iowa readers of the *Omaha World-Herald* only enhanced it. By adulthood, I hated

Iowa as much as Oklahoma, Colorado, Miami, and Florida State –
the Sworn Enemies – and gladly drank in the sweet, delicious
schadenfreude when they lost.

If you think about it, those are some pretty heavy hitters for the
Hawks to be mingling with. And it must really say something about
the depth of my antipathy toward Iowa football that I'd continue to
root against the Hawks even as Hayden Fry's on-field talent inevitably dwindled and the team's struggles grew. Sure, Iowa had had its
moments over the last dozen years, snagging a couple Rose Bowl
berths and finishing somewhere in the Top 20 once in a while. But
the Hawks were predestined to be a gridiron ham-n-egger, a middle-
of-the-pack Plain Jane. It was rooted in their identity: Analysts used
to say the Big 10's overall strength could be gauged by how good Iowa
was, basically saying the Hawkeyes were just average, and always
would be.

I suppose I thought – or maybe just hoped – this reality would
have beaten Hawkeye backers into submission. No such luck. The
black and gold in Iowa City was as pervasive as the red in Lincoln,
maybe even worse. Men, women, and children decorated themselves
in school colors. Every other business had "Hawk-I" or "Big 10" in its
name, while the local high school team proudly called itself the Little
Hawks. And the most popular bumper sticker in town was a picture
of the Hawkeye symbol with a rose in its beak, brazenly proclaiming,
"We Shall Return."

After about a month of watching this, a few questions came to
mind. Why was everyone so wound up about a team that, in the long
run, stood no chance in hell of ever winning anything? Didn't people
realize playing .500 ball and going to the Poulan Weed Whacker Bowl
wasn't exactly a reason to leap from their chairs? Why was their only
goal to play in – merely *play* in, not win – the boring old Rose Bowl,
which hadn't crowned a national champ since the middle of the
Pleistocene Epoch? And where, exactly, did the pride come from in
merely being a member of the Big 10? Just a few months removed
from watching Nebraska come a hair's breadth from claiming the
national championship in Miami, I found all of this a bit narrow-
minded.

Perhaps, I thought in a moment of misguided lucidity, fan fervor
wasn't directly proportional to the success of the team. Maybe Iowa
followers were the type of people you sometimes heard about who

stuck with their team through thick and thin – in this case, mostly thin. And perhaps, I reasoned, it was one thing to back a team that guns for the national title every year but another thing entirely to slip into Hawkeye gear week after week fully knowing your club was as relevant as a hip-hop artist holding a musical instrument. This was a different breed of football fan, a group seemingly content with the fact they simply *had* a team, and their squad was cut from that leather-helmeted, buzz-cut, pep-rally-and-bonfire-boola-boola cloth. As such, they operated with very little sense of urgency, mission, or purpose, at least compared to Cornhusker fans. NU fans would leave Memorial Stadium wondering if that day's performance would be good enough to win a Sears Trophy. Iowa fans would leave Kinnick knowing they were either better or worse than that day's opponent – nothing more.

Did this make them better fans? Whoa, whoa, whoa. I wasn't about to go that far. No, I concluded, this made Hawkeye fans sort of silly – or at the very least, provincial and myopic enough to believe such a letter-sweatered brand of football was still pertinent in this day and age. So I silently loathed them and was annoyed by them but allowed them to have their fun, safe in the knowledge I came from a far superior place that dealt in much more important matters than how to win the big game over grand old foes like Minnesota or Northwestern.

But by August those feelings gave way to a sharp and heavy sense of displacement. The familiar late-summer rituals – the opening of fall camp, the release of the preseason polls, the buildup of the early season hype – were taking shape, but for the first time something was askew. The Sunday sports sections were filled with banner headlines about the upcoming football season, all right, but they were about the Hawks' chances at finishing in the top half of the Big 10, not the annual report about the Big Red's backup long-snapper.

Wading through this, my psychic pull toward Lincoln became tremendous and insatiable; I found a short story on the Cornhuskers' preparations for the upcoming Kickoff Classic against West Virginia shoved into the corner of an inside page, but it said nothing of value. It was just some wire story slapped in to fill the section. I felt like Kevin Costner's character in *Dances with Wolves*, manning a remote outpost in the middle of nowhere, and the only other sentient beings were completely oblivious to the modern world.

Well, thank God for television, specifically the American Broadcasting Company, official home of the Kickoff Classic. Nebraska, who returned the core of the team that had flirted with immortality nine months earlier, was ranked fourth, while the rebuilding Mountaineers checked in at No. 24. Better yet, the Kickoff Classic was one of only a few college ballgames on that weekend, so there was no chance of ABC pre-empting it for a Big 10 game. And for that I was extremely thankful.

Even more gratifying, though, was the first camera shot of Dr. Tom and my Huskers as they made their way out of the tunnel at Giants Stadium. There was Tommie, there was Brook. There was Lawrence, Christian, Donta, and Dwayne. After being bombarded for months with Herky Hawk, Hayden Fry, and "We're Gonna Fight-Fight-Fight for Iowa," I greeted the sight of our towering, gum-chewing coach jogging onto the field with a pack of white helmets bobbing up and down behind him as a long-lost friend.

For the next four hours, I pulled the game around me like a blanket, watching in comfort and satisfaction as Nebraska blasted West Virginia into tiny atomic particles. The Blackshirts were simply unbudgeable – it was if defensive coordinator Charlie McBride had conjured up an invisible force field at the line of scrimmage, and the Mountaineers kept running directly into it, bouncing off, and falling onto their cans. Meanwhile, Tommie Frazier was galloping loose into the West Virginia secondary, bolting for three easy touchdowns. Sophomore Lawrence Phillips tacked on a 100-yard outing of his own, and the Cornhuskers looked like they were picking up where they had left off. The final count was Nebraska 31, West Virginia 0, but it wasn't nearly that close.

The next day, the lead story in the local sports section was about Iowa's season opener being just six days away. The Cornhuskers' win had made the section front, and this time they'd even splurged and tacked on a one-column black-and-white photograph of Frazier. I gobbled down this morsel as if it were my last meal on Earth, but I knew it was only delaying the inevitable. Soon enough it would be Monday, and I would be back at my station guarding my barren outpost, surrounded by football fans but at the same time very alone.

Fever Rising

NEBRASKA 24, COLORADO 7 – OCTOBER 29, 1994

After living away from Nebraska for awhile, you start to wonder if the place really exists or if it was maybe just an incredibly boring dream you once had. If you don't regularly seek out news from home or stay connected to the state through friends and family, Nebraska can sort of just fade away if you let it.

It can happen much more easily than you think. Nebraska is already invisible to the rest of the country, which finds little social, cultural, and political relevance here, so you hear virtually nothing about it in the national media. The only time you see the state on the network news is after some gargantuan tornado rips through. Otherwise, there's not a lot of reason to talk about the place. Nebraska's just sort of there, in the nation's blind spot, serving no compelling purpose except to keep Iowa, Colorado, South Dakota, and Kansas from running into one another.

It's uninteresting, I suppose, because it's unchanging. The pace is slow and movement slight. In all honesty, the state motto should probably be switched to something more accurate, like "Nebraska: Same As It Ever Was." But that'll never happen, because everyone knows the state motto is "The Good Life" and has been for years. To change it now would be . . . well, it would be a change, and we've already covered how little of that happens in Nebraska.

Still, for those of us who move away, the fact that Nebraska is set in its ways can be sort of comforting. You know that while you are off foraging around the outside world, through mountains, oceans, valleys, or deserts and living Where Big Things Happen, back home things are as eternally unbending as Tom Osborne's playbook. There's a certain stability in knowing when you return for a visit everything will look, sound, and feel exactly how you remember it. That makes the place more romantic and inviting, I suppose. It's sort of like how Valentino's, which makes decent but not great pizza, becomes mouth-wateringly legendary when you suddenly find yourself hundreds of miles from Lincoln and in need of a late-night snack. Even if you can't have it right then, it's important to know

89

Val's will be there when you return, as it always has been, just as you remember it.

Nebraska football is the Grand High Poobah of this feeling. Over the years, I've met hundreds of transplanted Nebraskans, many of whom didn't give a crap about Husker football when they lived there but became gigantic Cornhusker fans upon moving away. Why? Because after they left, they promptly recognized just how much of their lives were intertwined with the football team, whether they realized it or not. In a state where nothing changes, it's the constant above all constants.

There are other things that are uniquely Nebraskan that can make you homesick, of course – the license plates with county numbers on them, waterskiing at Lake McConaughy, scarfing down a Runza, rocking out at Comstock – but none of them can hope to match the Cornhuskers' significant pull. Plus, living halfway across the country, you can't summon up a Runza with a flick of the switch on your Panasonic. But you can do that with the Huskers. If you've got the time and the resources, the Big Red can be in your living room every Football Saturday, giving you a chance to see a slice of your homeland on the small screen. So for me, just like thousands of expatriates, the Huskers became the sole conduit to connect with home and pretty much the only way to retain a sense of definition and origin.

And, though I didn't think it was possible, I became an even *bigger* Husker fan after leaving Nebraska. In the fall of 1994 the best place to find me on Saturdays was barreling west on Interstate 80, looking for a good spot to pick up the game. My car radio would be tuned to 1110 AM and my ears would be peeled as I tried to distinguish through indecipherable static just who the hell had the ball. I also became intimately familiar with the sports ticker on CNN's *Headline News*, which gave updates of the games around the nation while they were in progress. It used to arrange the scores alphabetically by conference; Jesus knows how many things Kathy said to me that fell on deaf ears because the Big East scores were getting ripe on the bottom of my screen, and that meant the Big 8 ones were next.

Perhaps in my most resourceful stroke, I studied ABC's regional TV coverage map and deduced the cut-off between where they showed Big 10 and Big 8 games was probably about one hundred miles to my west. This was how in mid-October, when Nebraska went to Manhattan and whipped sixteenth-ranked Kansas State 17-6 behind backup quarterbacks Matt Turman and Brook Berringer, I found myself sitting alone in a dark tavern in Grinnell, Iowa, staring at the TV and tipping the pub's owner generously for the beer he wasn't supposed to be selling me because his joint didn't open until five. But it was worth it; I got to see one of the season's biggest victories, not to mention Troy Dumas pick off a pass from that relentless complainer Chad May and nearly run it back for 6 points. These are the lengths you go to when you live away. But luckily the game of the year – between Nebraska and the mighty Colorado Buffaloes in Lincoln – would be nationally televised, and I wouldn't have to drive anywhere to see it.

Few outside Nebraska gave the Cornhuskers any hope against the fearsome Colorado squad, which featured fistfuls of high-round NFL draft picks on both sides of the line. The Buffs were ranked second, one spot higher than NU, and had rung up seven straight victories behind the plowhorse runs of their Heisman frontrunner, Rashaan Salaam, not to mention a once-in-a-lifetime marvel of a catch by Michael Westbrook to beat the Michigan Wolverines in Ann Arbor. But even without the so-called Miracle at Michigan, the Buffs were a walking *SportsCenter* highlight. So the national consensus was that the Cornhuskers, perennial chokers who peed down their legs at the sight of any real competition, were in deep crap – and would have been even if they hadn't lost super-quarterback Tommie Frazier because of blood clots weeks earlier. Now, with the unadorned Brook Berringer at the controls, the Huskers were cooked.

Not this time. When I and a few other Husker fans gathered to watch the game at the Sports Column in downtown Iowa City, it was apparent something extraordinary was about to take place in Lincoln. It's difficult to explain, this sensation. It usually comes from how the Cornhuskers carry themselves during pregame warm-ups. And in this case, the Big Red was flying so high they practically needed clearance from the FAA before kickoff. Needless to say, I liked our chances.

On that late October day, Nebraska was inspired and inspiring. And the Huskers didn't just beat the Buffaloes, they slaughtered them. The Blackshirts swarmed over Salaam each time he touched the ball and terrorized CU quarterback Kordell Stewart on every snap. The mighty Buffaloes didn't convert a third down all day. Against NU's stalwart D, the Buffs' high-powered attack was useless.

They couldn't run. They couldn't throw. The only thing they did with any consistency was punt. With every thwarted drive, Stewart's wince grew wider as he trotted toward the CU sideline. It was a masterpiece by Charlie McBride.

But most of all, this was Berringer's day. In just his fourth start, the junior from Goodland, Kansas, engineered the victory with the deft skill of a veteran. In sixty golden minutes, Berringer went from no-frills backup to the maestro of a national-title contender.

His shining moment came in the third quarter with the Cornhuskers ahead 17-0 and the ball at the Colorado 30. Berringer took the snap, sprinted to his right, then stepped back and lofted a strike to wide-open Eric Alford. No. 88 gathered it in, rumbled past a pair of puzzled CU defenders and waltzed into the South end zone without anyone laying a hand on him. As he did, Alford thrust his index finger skyward, indicating what the national pollsters would confirm the following day – Nebraska was, once again, No. 1 in all the land.

As those final, saccharine-sweet seconds ticked off the clock, the fans overran the fences, spilled onto the field and rode the goal posts to the turf. Behind them, Memorial Stadium's big orange scoreboard flashed a simple message: "The Luck Stopped Here." Four hundred miles away from the center of a suddenly boundless universe, our tiny red commune also celebrated in a flurry of hugs, high-fives, and those eternally optimistic decrees that gush out after a big victory, when everything seems easy and absolutely nothing impossible: *We're gonna head back to Miami. We're gonna get another shot at it. We're gonna finish business.*

It would have been nice to stay a while longer, but Hawkeye fans had started to pour in to watch Iowa play Purdue. Outnumbered, we squeezed our way out of the Sports Column and onto the city streets. We walked along proudly in a small, smiling red pack, secure in each other's company – and in the knowledge that back home, everything was the same as it ever was.

At Last

NEBRASKA 24, MIAMI 17 – JANUARY 1, 1995

When I was a kid, my brother-in-law Kevin gave my dad a videotape of the Game of the Century for Christmas. He might as well have given it to me. For two months in January and February 1987, I watched the tape religiously, memorizing the plays, the calls from the broadcast booth, and the players and their mannerisms. Our vcr, which was so large it could have been used for modest housing when we were finished with it, also displayed the number of frames on the tape it was playing, unlike today's much more practical minute-and-second models. During lulls in the game I'd sometimes watch the numerals tick upward, remembering exactly where on the tape the biggest plays were.

Once, while watching the game's final scoring drive, I realized the frame-counter was around 1,950 and climbing. There was no comma in the number, though, so the ascending figures looked more like a tour through the twentieth century: 1961, 1962, 1963, and so on. Meanwhile, back on the tv screen, Jerry Tagge, Johnny Rodgers, and Jeff Kinney were closing in on the end zone, ready to finish their march into nirvana.

I kept one eye on the screen and the other on the vcr counter, because I took all this to be a sign – a developing prophecy of sorts that would contain the answer to the most burning question on every Nebraskan's mind: *When will Nebraska win the national championship again?* I knew that in mere moments, Kinney would be crashing into the end zone, and I concluded that when it happened, the number on the vcr display would signify the year that they'd next win it all.

I was disappointed to see, as the Huskers broke the huddle, the number 1987 roll by. So did 1988, 1989, and 1990, and they were only getting into their three-point stances. Eventually, NU snapped the ball, Tagge turned and handed to Kinney, and, shoulder pads flapping, No. 35 made his famous leap. I watched for the officials to signal a touchdown, then pressed Pause on the vcr's remote control.

And you know what the counter read? Well, 1994 would be a good guess, and it probably would make this story better. But the magical counter read 2029.

2029. I would not experience true joy until I was nearly ready to retire. So, in a flash of brilliance I decided it wasn't a sign after all. I rewound the tape, put it back in its case, and didn't think of it again.

Actually, that's a lie. I recalled the vcr's divination later that year, when the Oklahoma Sooners crushed our dreams of a national title by whipping us in Lincoln. And it came to mind in the seasons after that, as my heart was repeatedly broken by the likes of Darian Hagan,

Eric Bienemy, Steve Walsh, and Scott Bentley. As proud as I was to watch NU stand toe-to-toe with mighty Florida State in the Orange Bowl, it was beginning to dawn on me the vcr might have been right. I might not live to see Nebraska *ever* win the national championship again.

The last time Nebraska pulled it off, I had been too young to appreciate it; in fact, I was still in diapers. I've been told that Dad bought a color tv for the Orange Bowl and that we had the Richardsons over to watch Nebraska slap Alabama. Over the next twenty-three years, that team's reputation as the charmed group of Huskers who could close the deal had grown into the stuff of legend. All other Big Reds that followed were destined to never be able to measure up to the '71 squad.

But in the fall of 1994, I let myself believe again. With Tommie Frazier seemingly out for the year, the team had rallied around Brook Berringer. After dispatching Colorado on Homecoming, the Cornhuskers clubbed Kansas, defeated Iowa State, and polished off Oklahoma (and sealed the fate of Gary Gibbs, who could never live up to Barry Switzer's formidable legacy in Norman) to finish the regular season top-ranked. Nebraska wasn't blowing teams apart but had acquired that unmistakable energy that seemed to form around a legitimate title contender. NU also had a massive offensive line – the Pipeline – that blocked out the sun, and a defense that had nobly stepped up after Frazier's injury to give Berringer time to find his sea legs. Just one final hurdle to jump, I thought, and we could plunge head-first into the sweet thereafter.

That feeling lasted until the bowl bids went out, and Nebraska learned it would travel to Miami to play the hometown Hurricanes. The mention of that hideous name melted my season-long excitement into anger. How many times were we going to have to play these bastards in their own backyard? The fury was followed by a sense of downright dread: Three times in the past decade Nebraska had faced the Hurricanes at the Orange Bowl, and three times had returned shocked, empty-handed, and demoralized. Miami, meantime, had won four national titles in that span. And in '94, the Canes possessed what some considered its best defense in school history, and that was really saying something.

I couldn't imagine Nebraska winning. I couldn't even picture what a victory over Miami might look like. I supposed it was achievable, of course, and when Kathy and I came home for Christmas I gave those who were wildly optimistic their due respect. Sometimes I even joined in, but inside I fortified myself for the probability of defeat. For the first time, I understood the thinking of those people preparing for their second marriages who pushed for prenuptial agreements: For the record, you smile and say how you're sure everything will be just fine, but inside you're saying, *I am simply not going to allow myself to get taken again.*

The morning of the game, the *Des Moines Register* had a story about Frazier, who had recovered in December and earned the start in the Orange Bowl. It also mentioned Warren Sapp, the Hurricanes' monstrous defensive tackle who was as mouthy as he was unblockable. We had some friends from Nebraska, including my buddy Michael, staying with us in Iowa City, and that night we all headed over to my co-worker Mindy's house to watch the game. Mindy, a Lincoln native, even made Runzas for the occasion, but I was too nervous to eat.

It didn't take long for my fears to be realized. I remember the sinking, icy sensation of seeing Miami, buoyed by its hometown fans, twice bolt to a 10-point lead. I watched helplessly as Osborne started Frazier, replaced him with Berringer, and then re-inserted Frazier near the end with the Huskers down 8. It wasn't working: Sapp flung Tommie for a 4-yard loss on No. 15's first play back, and then Frazier was stopped cold on third down. The Hurricanes pranced off the field, and it looked like the beginning of the end. Barely ten minutes were left.

The impending finality of it all left me hollow inside. I'd really fallen in love with this team. It had fought through blood clots, collapsed lungs, and who knows what else to make it back to that sandy, south-Florida field for one more shot at this impossible dream, and dammit, it wasn't going to be enough. Still, I resolved to be proud of them, because for one spectacular autumn my Cornhuskers had mixed precise execution with an unquenchable desire to create a team whose whole was greater than the sum of its parts. It had been a beautiful thing to watch come together, even if it was destined to splinter apart in the end.

But in a stirring string of events, Nebraska found itself at the Miami 15, and seconds later, Frazier put the ball in fullback Cory Schlesinger's hands. No. 40 slipped past the line, leaped over a Hurricane at the 5, and remarkably, bounded into the end zone. Then Frazier fired a bullet to Eric Alford for 2 points, and the game was tied. At some point during all of this, I turned to Michael. He was looking at me, holding up four fingers. Then he asked: "Do you believe?"

Suddenly, I did. And the Cornhuskers rewarded me in the greatest way possible. In a drive that gets sweeter every time I think of it, NU pounded its way into history by putting on a clinic on Nebraska football. Lawrence Phillips off the right side. A timing-route catch by Reggie Baul. Frazier on the option for 25 big ones. Phillips again, up the gut for 7 more. Phillips on the stretch play to the right. Frazier on an option again, for 6 yards and a crucial first down. And then, in the fifty-eighth minute of the sixty-first Orange Bowl, Frazier slipped the ball to Schlesinger again, and the kid from Duncan charged straight ahead, caught a block from Abdul Muhammad, and tumbled onto colored turf. The next thing I knew, I was running down the hall away from the living room, fists pummeling the air, screaming something unintelligible. Darian Hagan, Eric Bienemy, Steve Walsh, Scott Bentley – they were all behind me now. Far, far behind.

Then, those things I couldn't picture before began to play out: The Huskers in the victory formation, *in the Orange Bowl*. Frazier going down on one knee. Dr. Tom receiving congrats from his players, his assistants, even one of the chain-gang guys. Dr. Tom getting Gatoraded, having a "Big Red 1994 National Champs" hat slapped on his head, and being interviewed by John Dockery while flash bulbs burst. The Big Red leaving the field, helmets held high in triumph. I'm not ashamed to say I wept like a day-old infant at the sight of all this, because I know of much manlier men who broke down into even bigger piles of Jell-O at this sight. At last it had finally happened, and no emotion seemed too big.

Our celebration carried on into the early morning. When we finally got back to our apartment I found a half-dozen phone messages, all from Iowa City friends calling with congratulations. The next day, I must've spent three hours on the phone chatting with people who thought immediately of calling me after the Cornhuskers' win. That's something only Husker football can do. I mean, lots of people know I love U2 and are aware that I'm a devoted fan of their music, but no one has ever floated me a congratulatory call after the band wins a Grammy. I really dig the thought that when some of my friends see the Big Red on TV, I'm the first person they think of. In a way that gives me an even bigger stake in the team.

That week my folks mailed me two videotapes. The first was a copy of NBC's game broadcast, the second, local news coverage of the team's reception at the Devaney Sports Center. To a man, the players and coaches stepped to the podium and declared they hadn't won the Orange Bowl just for the team, they'd won it for the whole state of Nebraska.

They weren't saying this just to get some cheap applause. Nor had they come up with the cliché proposal of dedicating the victory to the fans like some kind of game ball. No, they were merely recognizing the obvious: This championship belonged to all of us. Over the years, we'd worked hard and put in the time and effort, and suffered through all those cataclysmic near-misses too. That's what made this all the more sweet.

Kent Pavelka said it best during the game's radio broadcast, when he was opining about the win being the end of a quest by the players, the football program, and, yes, the fans. It might sound absurd anywhere else to give the fans that much credit, but Husker fandom is much different than at other schools, which can only dream of having the border-to-border community of support that exists in Nebraska. That brings us closer to the team, somehow; and we know when the Big Red wins a big one – in this case, *the* big one – the players are the ones who get to hoist the trophy and wear the rings. But they do it knowing they're not alone. We're a part of them, and they're a part of us.

I guess that's why, while watching my worn-out tape of that most cherished, most special victory for the thousandth time, I still get blubbery – and exhausted, as if I'd played the game myself and left it all out there on the field. But most of all, I'm really, really proud, because I'd like to think I, too, really accomplished something that night.

Trouble

NEBRASKA 49, KANSAS STATE 25 – OCTOBER 21, 1995

Contrary to popular belief, it's actually possible to learn a thing or two by following college football. In particular, the game helps you with geography: The capital of Louisiana is, of course, Baton Rouge, home of the LSU Tigers. But the capital of Oregon is Salem, *not* Eugene, where the Ducks play ball. Mount Nittany is in Pennsylvania. There's a place called Death Valley in Clemson, South Carolina, in addition to the one in California. Texas and Oklahoma are divided by the Red River. The Chippewa Indians used to roam the central part of Michigan. And Manhattan, Kansas, is full of rednecks. Though I suppose that last one goes without saying.

But those are just a bunch of random facts, which might come in handy in a game of Trivial Pursuit and little else. True wisdom, of course, comes from experience, challenging your own assumptions and beliefs, and examining both sides of an issue. To that end, it's been said that holding two contradictory ideas in your head is a sign of first-rate intelligence. In the fall of 1995, it was practically a necessity.

It started when Lawrence Phillips, in one of his frequent fits of fury, scaled a wall to his ex-girlfriend's apartment, crawled inside, beat her, and then dragged her down three flights of stairs. For weeks a media firestorm rained down on Lincoln, the likes of which we'd never seen – in addition to blow-by-blow coverage of the Phillips case, a handful of other incidents involving current or former players came to the fore. Then the entire nation took notice, mouths agape, as Tom Osborne threw Phillips off the team, then amended his punishment to an indefinite suspension, and eventually announced he could come back if he met certain conditions. Nine months after being the toast of college football, the Cornhuskers were now simply toast.

When the smoke finally cleared, all that was left was the image of a tiny town on the Plains and a football program completely out of control. And that was just about the lousiest feeling in the whole world. It wasn't just my co-workers' constant gibes. And it wasn't because scoffs had replaced the kindly nods I once received when my fellow Iowans saw me in my Husker red. And certainly it wasn't because this news somehow took me by surprise – I was just a couple years out of school, after all; I knew what football players were capable of. What made me feel crummy, actually, was that I had mixed feelings about the whole mess.

Allow me to explain. If you're a fan of the Nebraska Cornhuskers, you typically gravitate toward one of two camps. The first group is full of old-school idealists. They hold the football program to a letter-sweater, halcyon-days-of-yore standard and trust in the myth of the Nebraska Ideal – that our team not only wins but wins the right way, with liberty and justice for all, amen. The second group, meanwhile, just wants to win. Period. More vicarious than their counterparts, they think the tribalism, communal fervor, and warm fuzziness Nebraska football creates is nice but not worth a bucket of warm spit if the team doesn't pulverize the opponent to dust on a week-in, week-out basis.

The Cornhuskers' legal woes didn't create this central split in the fan base, of course. It merely highlighted something that existed long before Lawrence Phillips, Running Back, became Lawrence Phillips, Destroyer of Worlds. While one group claps for opponents and thinks *More Than Winning* should be added to the New Testament, the other boos its own quarterback and believes that over the last forty years Nebraska has had only five truly successful seasons. Neither group is particularly fond of the other, and both shape too much of their respective ideologies on emotion, as sports fans tend to do. And so neither can grasp the upper hand in their battle of wills – not in '68 when Bob Devaney was under fire, not in the debate following Osborne's decision to go for two, and certainly not during the long, strange autumn of 1995.

Me? I was stuck somewhere in the middle, which was precisely what led to my moral uneasiness. Obviously, I felt terrible for the victims, who deserved justice. I was also angry at Lawrence Phillips for bringing shame upon my alma mater and wanted him gone, if for no other reason than to protect my university from further harm. I felt bad for the hundred or so other players who probably hadn't even done as much as crossed a street against the light but who were now all being branded as goons. But at the same time, I worried about how it was going to affect their on-the-field performance. Could they overcome the distractions and keep winning? Could Phillips's replacements carry the load? Would the national pollsters punish NU for their transgressions by voting Nebraska lower in the polls? How would this affect recruiting? Could Lawrence return in time for the Colorado game?

My double-mindedness was a genuine dilemma. I'm sure I'm not the only one who felt this way either. In a vacuum the choice would have been perfectly clear: Throw the bum out. We're high on personal responsibility here in Red America, after all. But Lawrence was a *Husker*, man. And the team was a machine, gunning for another national title. We'd reworked our beliefs simply for the sake of another undefeated season. Until then, it had never been an option to fulfill my needs as a fan at the expense of others, and it didn't feel very good knowing that's exactly what was happening.

Complicating the matter was that by late October, it was clear Nebraska was a powerhouse. With the imperturbable Tommie Frazier running the show and an overwhelming offensive line blowing Peterbilt-size holes into opposing defenses, Nebraska lit up scoreboards like the White House Christmas tree. On the other side of the ball, the Blackshirts quite literally had no weakness, shutting down every offense they faced. There wasn't a lot of poetry in the Huskers' victories, but it was hard not to be in awe of their sheer power.

The day NU hosted eighth-ranked and unbeaten Kansas State, I returned to Lincoln to watch. My friend Jeff and I sat in Memorial Stadium's southeast corner and witnessed the Cornhuskers systematically break down the Wildcats that afternoon. This was the contest, you may remember, when Mike Rucker hit a KSU special-teamer so hard the poor Wildcat's helmet flew into the air, quite possibly with his head still inside. This was also the day wunderkind freshman Ahman Green became a man, or more accurately, showed everyone he had been one for some time. After catching a shovel pass from Frazier inside the K-State 5, Green appeared to be wrangled to the turf by a couple of Wildcats. But somehow he kept his knees from touching the ground, and in one powerful motion, No. 30 ripped away from their grasp, sprung upright and high-stepped backward into the end zone. It was brilliant.

Leaving the stadium, Jeff and I recalled the pregame talk about how Nebraska would struggle with Kansas State's top-ranked defense. I guess if you were Bill Snyder, you could take a small measure of satisfaction knowing that your mighty D held the Huskers' rushing attack out of the end zone the whole afternoon. But Frazier threw for four touchdowns, and the NU defense and special teams each picked up scores too. That was the thing with this incredible team: It could destroy you in just about any way imaginable. In many ways these Huskers were the essence of everything Tom Osborne had labored over the years to build. Everything they did – run, pass, kick, tackle – they carried out with ruthless efficiency and a precision that led to the calculated destruction of every single opponent who had the misfortune of being on the schedule.

That's the enduring image I like to keep of that great, unbeaten team. I remember the magnificent option quarterback, the damn-near impenetrable defense, and play after superhuman play. In my mind, I've even condensed the moral debate that raged that fall into a nice, neat statement – *what Lawrence Phillips did was wrong, but so was the treatment we got from the national media.* Ten years of rationalization, rolled into one sentence.

Today it's practically a cliché for a Cornhusker football player to make headlines because of trouble with the law. Whenever it happens, Husker fans dutifully break into their two divergent groups and start the debate once more. And true to form, I start to feel conflicted all over again. But if there's one thing I have learned since the autumn of 1995, it's this: No matter what group you're in, no matter where your moral compass lies in regards to the "Cornvicts," you're going to be affected. If you're a Nebraskan, then you've pledged allegiance to a team no one else can stand, in no small part because of the players' off-field antics. So we have adopted the stance of besieged minority: We become needlessly emotional at every slight, real or imagined. Our thin-skinned reputation precedes us, as does our over-sensitivity to any type of criticism, and we genuinely believe the media conspire against us. This is what Lawrence Phillips has wrought.

It's too bad, really, that football has affected our lives in this manner. Growing up, I often wished the game's straight-line, clear-cut nature could translate to real life. On the field, there wasn't much gray area, not a lot of room for spin. You either won or you lost; plays either worked or failed. Outside that green rectangle, life was often puzzling and muddled and awkward and filled with conflicts that didn't always have clear resolutions. In 1995 real life seeped onto the field instead, bringing all its complexities and confusion with it, and I didn't know exactly how to handle it. Had the Cornhuskers been losers on the field, my feelings probably would have been clearer, but week-in and week-out they kept defying the odds, critics, and the laws of chance. I told myself this was something to support, but not entirely. One minute I would run to their defense, the next I would simply run away, embarrassed that I was associated with them. And that sums up that year pretty well, come to think of it. It was wonderful, but it was also awful.

Priceless

When I was in sixth grade, I read a great line in *Sports Illustrated*'s recap of the 1983 Orange Bowl about how Nebraska fans would ride bareback on a camel just to see their team play. Now when I see a stadium gushed in red at a Husker road game, I can't help but envision a long line of furry beige creatures trudging their way across miles of barren terrain, and on top are intensely determined people in red. They bounce along slowly, hoping not to fall while they read their maps and check their watches every two or three minutes. And, of course, each camel is wearing a red-and-white shawl and is equipped with a gas-powered grill, red lawn chairs, a large cooler, a nineteen-inch television, and a DirecTV dish with an ESPN Game-Plan subscription.

It's astounding how fast a Nebraskan can go from tightwad to spendthrift as soon as a big red *N* is added to the equation. If the Unicameral was really serious about the state budget deficit, it would simply slap a 10 percent tax on purchases of Husker junk, and within a month there would be enough of a surplus in the state coffers to buy Wyoming. Which is sort of odd, given the average Nebraskan's attitude toward spending – in general, we're a pretty thrifty bunch. I suppose this is because like most Midwesterners, we're inherently modest, and we're uncomfortable if we stand out from the rest of the pack. There is definite social pressure not to put on airs. If a resident of a small town drove down Main Street in a brand-new Mercedes, for example, he'd be greeted with scowls of disapproval. So we save our money for the essentials, things that won't be perceived as frivolous.

This tendency must come from our pioneering ancestors, who had to make do with whatever they had. There were no vinyl-siding salesmen waiting for them when they arrived in Nebraska; hell, there weren't even any trees. So they built homes out of sod, tended to their little corner of the world, and lived very basic, unassuming lives. Then in the late 1800s, football started being played over at State U, and the local dry-goods stores began having a run on red ribbons. Next thing you knew, people were driving carriages for miles to see the team play. To this day, whenever our Bugeater gene meets our homesteader gene, the Bugeater gene wins in a rout.

I figure that between game tickets, travel expenses, subscriptions to various sports media, clothing, and other assorted Huskerphernalia, I've dropped more than fifteen thousand dollars in my adult life to feed my obsession for Cornhusker football. There are a lot of goods, services, and generally life-improving things I could have attained with that kind of scratch – a new roof for my house, for example. However, as pleasant as having my home's interior protected from the elements might be, *a new roof will never help Nebraska get to a good bowl game.* It's that simple. Besides, I've found that packing the holes in my roof with sod is quite effective.

Moreover, buying into the Cornhuskers is another way I, well, buy into the Cornhuskers. Like all fans, I would like to think at the end of the day I have more invested in the team than just my mouth. Getting season tickets and traveling to Pasadena, Tempe, or (ugh) Shreveport shows I have devoted more than simple emotion to the Big Red. I've put my money where my mouth is, and there's a strong feeling of accomplishment that goes with that (entitlement too – my dollars also buy my right to be indignant or outraged, and they validate my complaints about play calling and feed my suspicion I could make better personnel decisions than the coaches). Why else would Memorial Stadium's sellout streak be lauded with just as much pomp as the streaks the team creates? Why else would you commemorate one of the worst special-teams disasters in Nebraska football history by making a "Sea of Red" poster showing Notre Dame Stadium filled with Nebraska fans? Why do we go along with the silly appeals for Red Outs for big home games?

Because it's the only way we know to break down that invisible barrier between the stands and the field. By merely showing up and shouting, we think we're able to help the team, from goading the opponents into false starts to impressing a coveted recruit to being a financial bargaining chip for the athletic director as he's shopping the Huskers around for a decent bowl bid. Sometimes, we even think we can help our quarterback find his receiver, our defensive ends beat their blockers, and our tailbacks slash through tackles. The feeling is hard to explain and even harder to quantify, but everyone who goes through the turnstiles wearing red knows how it feels.

Nothing thrills us more than when we hear Nebraska's players speak of our allegiance and how they draw inspiration from it. It was clear this was in play when the top-ranked Cornhuskers ran out of the tunnel in Tempe to play Florida for the 1995 national championship. Liberated by NU's Orange Bowl triumph a year earlier, many confident Husker fans had snapped up tickets for the '96 Fiesta Bowl nearly a year in advance. As a result Nebraska played a bowl game in a stadium saturated in red. It wasn't Miami in the Orange Bowl or LSU in the Sugar Bowl or even Houston in the Cotton Bowl. For one evening Tempe, Arizona, looked as much like Lincoln as humanly possible.

I did my part, making the trek to Tempe with Kathy, my mom, and my middle sister, Kristy, who in early December had scrounged up four tickets in Section 34, Row 40, for the bargain-basement price of three hundred dollars apiece. At the time, that was roughly a week's pay. When offered two tickets, I didn't even let Kristy finish asking before taking them. I just opened my wallet and willingly watched as twenty-dollar bills flew west toward Omaha.

That's pretty much the way it was the whole trip. Thirty-five bucks for two "Nebraska Does the Desert" shirts from a vendor at a Phoenix mall? Sure. Five dollars for a bumper sticker with "Back to Back!" stamped on it in a gaudy script, bought off a hawker making his rounds at a Scottsdale bar the night before the game? No problem. Resorting to the Visa for a commemorative hat, pin, game program, and bag of bite-size Tostitos, all emblazoned with the Fiesta Bowl logo? Yes, yes, yes, and . . . hell, yes. I didn't care. I wanted it all.

It's safe to say we all got our money's worth that evening. In what was billed as the first college Super Bowl, the Huskers were matched against No. 2 Florida, a high-flying, unbeaten squad with the most sophisticated passing attack in college football. The Gators cruised through the rugged Southeastern Conference on the howitzer of Danny Wuerffel, the square-jawed triggerman of the "Fun N Gun" offense, and with the scheming of their maniacal coach, the eminently hateable Steve Spurrier. The oddsmakers picked NU by the slightest of margins – they, along with everyone else, expected the irresistible force and the immovable object to have a pretty good go at each other. And at the start of the second quarter, it looked like the pundits were going to be right: Florida converted a short passing attack and a pick off Tommie Frazier to forge a 10-6 lead.

What's the correct metaphor for what came next? Nebraska's emphatic 29-point second quarter, in which the Blackshirts and the Big Red's bullish offensive line seized absolute control of the game, was an explosion, a flurry, a demolition. But none of those descriptions lives up to the transcendent brilliance of that quarter, when a great team became the Greatest Team Ever by willing itself to another level and making the extraordinary ordinary. Moments into the quarter, Lawrence Phillips tore through the middle of the line, shook off two tacklers, juked another, and blasted down the sideline for a 42-yard touchdown. Next thing we knew, Jamel Williams sacked Wuerffel for a safety, and Ahman Green crashed into the end zone for another score. By the time Florida staggered off the field at halftime, it was 35-10, and it was over.

In the stands the second half was a long, festive coronation. Only once – when Florida scored near the end of the third quarter to cut the lead to 24 – was there any twinge of doubt about the game's outcome. That doubt was erased seconds later by Tommie Frazier. On the last play of the third quarter, No. 15 ran a simple option play to the right, then turned upfield. He was looking for an opening in the defense and found immortality instead. When it was over, seven Florida defenders had tried to drag Frazier down, but they could only watch in awe – along with the rest of us – as he powered through the tangle of orange, white, and blue, broke into the clear along the sideline, and rumbled 75 yards for a score.

The Run, as it is simply called, was Touchdown Tommie's last visit to the end zone in his amazing tenure at Nebraska. Many scrambled to affix the appropriate symbolism to the play: It was an emblem of Tommie Frazier's career; it was an exhibition of the lopsidedness of the game; it was a symbol of NU's resilience in the face of off-field controversy. I simply preferred to think of the Run as Frazier's final display of greatness, a supreme athlete getting one last chance to demonstrate his sheer will to win.

As the replay flickered across the big screens, I rose from my seat. All around was red as far as the eye could see, screaming and embracing and chanting and taking in the moment – the greatest moment in the greatest victory by the greatest team ever assembled. It was a spectacular feeling to be part of that, to see it, to revel in it, and to feel the communal delight of it all. I felt truly blessed to be there. A fan can spend decades, and thousands upon thousands of dollars, following his team, hoping to experience just a slice of what it was like in those golden moments following the Run. This complete and utter triumph is a kind of feeling you might have once in your life. I know how that feels – I felt it firsthand, and I simply can't put a price on that.

Baud to the Bone

NEBRASKA 65, COLORADO STATE 9 – SEPTEMBER 28, 1996

I'm addicted to Husker Internet message boards. There, I said it. Hours can melt away when I sink into that artificial realm where everyone is just as wonderfully and irrationally fixated on the Cornhuskers as I am (and sometimes even more so, if that's possible). By the time I'm done consuming every point, rebuttal, lament, or taunt the CyberCorn Circles have to offer, the clock has leaped forward in huge bounds. Suddenly it's dark outside, I'm back in front of my computer screen, and the ice in my glass has turned into a half-inch of liquid. So I get up and stretch, refill my Coke, maybe even do something constructive like feed the cat. Then I dive right back in to see what's new, because the boards change from second to second, you know, and I don't want to miss anything good.

That's the way it's been since 1996, when I first fired up my modem and pointed my cursor toward home. At the time I had no clue how vital the Web would be to me as a far-flung fan; all I really wanted was to be able to tell my co-workers I had e-mail. But soon I was navigating through the online Husker world and interacting with Nebraskans all over the face of the planet.

The Web also helped to stave off the pervasive Hawkeyeness of Iowa City. Black-and-gold fervor had risen steadily in the two years I had lived there because somehow Hayden Fry had resurrected Iowa from the brink of oblivion. As the new season approached, the excitement among the locals practically had an electromagnetic pulse. At the Sports Column, the regulars were daring to speak of (ooh! ahh!) a Big 10 title. Luckily, we got America Online in the nick of time, and I was saved from the madness, if just for a few hours each day, by the virtual Lincolnland inside my computer screen.

It was that connection to home that first pulled me in to the Husker message boards, but it was their ever-changing nature that hooked me – and continues to hook me to this day. You never really know what you're going to get when you log on. One minute the boards can resemble a newsroom, the next, a town hall meeting. Then they look like a pep rally or maybe a locker room or even a comedy club. In other words, they're a community unto themselves, full of like-minded Husker nuts, with pages upon pages of Big Red goodness that go on into infinity.

The good thing about message boards? They're an endless electronic haven where militant Big Red fans can bask 24/7 in their fanaticism. The bad thing about message boards? They're an endless electronic haven where militant Big Red fans can bask 24/7 in their fanaticism. In other words, like any addiction, they're both enjoyable and destructive. Their constantly morphing makeup makes them magical but also ensures that by the time a topic has been covered, it's been examined to absurd lengths. What could be a bigger waste of time than reading dozens of posts dissecting what Tom Osborne's record would have been in 1998 had he stayed on? Well, reading dozens of posts about what Frank Solich's record would have been in 2004 if he could have stayed on, that's what. I'm ashamed to admit I've done both. I can't help it. If it's about the Huskers, I must consume it.

I gorge myself on nearly all of the mini-dissertations in hopes of coming away with some tangible, useable thoughts and some kind of new perspective. But that rarely happens. I don't get a lot of nutrition from the CyberCorn Circles, just a lot of empty calories. I appreciate most posters' enthusiasm for the Huskers, of course, probably because I'm relieved to know I'm not the only one afflicted to such a frightening degree. But there's rarely very much to the discussions. The posts – choppy little ill-constructed blasts of passion – are too brief to create debates with very much depth or complexity. No one seems willing to give ground or take a point either, so before long all threads degenerate into a repetitious, predictable exchange, like an online Miller Lite commercial: *Less filling! Tastes great!*

Part of the message boards' problems have to do with the tone that has permeated the Internet. Because of anonymity and lack of proximity, message boards are not exactly the friendliest places in the world. A guy from Connecticut can flip someone from Chicago the cyber-finger and face no real ramifications. Even on a board inhabited by good-natured, corn-fed folk from Nebraska, most posters operate with a subtle disdain for one another. Or worse, they run in warring cliques and cults of personality. This general testiness can explode into a confrontation at a moment's notice, and usually does.

I know that when I sign on I become an extreme version of myself, and that annoys the hell out of people. I am a perpetual smartass; I come off as aloof and, in my weaker moments, condescending. I suspect when I encounter other posters online, I'm dealing with their super-selves as well. The assertive alpha male isn't as big of a knuckle-dragging troglodyte in real life, nor is the mousy milksop a ninety-pound weakling with no social life. Well, maybe he is. But the point is, the personality in every post seems to grow tenfold by the time it shows up on my screen.

Maybe that's why when taken collectively, Internet message boards appear to be a series of giant mood swings. Moments after a four-star quarterback commits to Lincoln, they're bursting with unbridled enthusiasm. Seconds later they crash to earth and are awash in doomsday prophecies when a coveted receiver out of California chooses USC. Nothing is taken in moderation. We're either at the top of peaks or the bottom of valleys. I picture the people on the other end sitting in front of their screens in their game outfits – hat, sweatshirt, earphones, red-and-white tiger-striped Zuba pants – reacting to the posts as if they were in the stands at Memorial Stadium, engulfed in a tight ballgame.

Research has shown that during a game, the testosterone level of the crowd rises in proportion to the excitement on the field. Online, the game never seems to end. That perpetual ire is often directed toward players and coaches and spawns cyber-rumors that become instant urban legends. I can only imagine how different Husker history would be if the Internet had been around in the late 1970s. Undoubtedly, a cantankerous fan frustrated with Osborne's inability to beat Oklahoma would have floated a rumor about him and some South Stadium intern, and that would've been it for the good doctor.

Thank goodness things moved slower then. But the Web's constant prattle has sped everything up and has bred an impatient demand for results, even when there's no opportunity to get them. In cyberspace, we expect a resolution to every perceived crisis within the hour. The problem is, in real space, Football Saturday comes but once a week.

In their second game of 1996, the top-ranked Huskers got shut out 19-0 by the Arizona State Sun Devils. The Cornhuskers' first defeat in twenty-seven games was as painful as it was shocking. Not only had it been twenty-three years since NU had been blanked in the regular season, but it had gotten beat by a crew it had pummeled 77-28 a year earlier. This grand and glorious implosion didn't sit well with anyone in red. Roughly 90 percent of the catastrophe was blamed on Scott Frost, Tommie Frazier's successor at quarterback, who spent most of the night looking slow and confused.

In Nebraska, there's always a tremendous sense of urgency following a loss, and it was magnified a million times over in the male-dominated online forums: In the hours after the loss, message boards raged with debate – over Frost's performance, over what went wrong on defense, over what was the biggest turning point in the game, over which Huskers got outplayed, and over what needed to be done to right the ship. "IMHO, we need to get this &^%$# thing fixed ASAP," one poster opined around 2 a.m. Sunday, exhibiting a startling grasp of the obvious.

Here is another way the Internet can be detrimental to your health: For the next four days, I spent nearly all my free time in front of my Macintosh, wallowing in the loss with other online fans. Before the Internet, I could reconcile a loss by the following Monday, Tuesday at the latest, if it were a particularly hairy defeat. But here it was, late on a Thursday night, and I still felt miserable. Logging off that evening, I was convinced Nebraska would never win another football game.

The phone rang. It was my friend Michael, who had joined us in Iowa City two years earlier to watch Nebraska win the Orange Bowl. He said he had two tickets to that Saturday's game against Colorado State. It took some convincing, but I eventually agreed to drive the five hours to Lincoln for the game. "God help 'em if they don't take their opening drive right down the field and score," I told him. "They might need to call up the National Guard to keep the peace."

Thankfully, DeAngelo Evans returned Colorado State's opening kickoff for a big gainer, and the Cornhuskers marched 62 yards in ten plays for a touchdown the first time they had the ball. In the sun-soaked stands, the 3-yard scoring pass from Frost to tight end Vershan Jackson was greeted more with relief than elation. Still, Ahman Green ran wild, Frost was a meticulous 13 of 18 passing, the Blackshirts shut down CSU, and lots of scrubs got to play. It was a quintessential Cornhusker ass-kicking, just what we needed after a long, unsettling week.

As Michael and I left the stadium, we saw Mike Minter and Mike Fullman walking north over the Tenth Street pedestrian bridge. Michael, who was a chemistry graduate assistant at the time, had taught a class with Minter in it one semester earlier, so we caught up with them and struck up a conversation. Minter said matter-of-factly that the ASU game had been a "wake-up call" and that the team was a little complacent until then. But now they were ready to stomp their way to St. Louis, host of the newly formed Big 12 Conference's title game, no problem. I remember little else about the conversation, except that Michael asked Minter about snagging a pro contract, which made Fullman chuckle. We talked with them to the bottom of the bridge, where we parted company.

I was struck at how level-headed and unflappable they both seemed – strangely calm and serene and kind of happy-go-lucky, as if that horrible debacle in the desert had never even happened. I figured if I had felt all week as if the world was ending, then the players naturally must have felt the same way. They probably just didn't have Internet access.

Blackshirts and Black Cats

NEBRASKA 45, MISSOURI 38 – NOVEMBER 8, 1997

There is a woman in Leawood, Kansas, who claims she can talk to angels. One day not too long ago, she drove up to Lincoln and offered, for a fee, to teach this divine art. Twenty-nine Lincolnites paid $111 each to sit in a semi-circle in a conference room at the Hampton Inn and spend a gorgeous June Saturday persuading Raphael, Gabriel, and Michael to drop by. It's unclear how many angels, if any, actually showed up or if they partook in the continental breakfast out in the lobby, but one woman reportedly saw a white tunnel, outstretched hands, and a white candle, so *something* must have been up. Another mentioned she didn't necessarily *see* any angels but did feel an energetic sensation wash over her. Still another proclaimed the session was a success because her headache had suddenly vanished – not to mention $111 from her billfold.

Now, you may chortle at all this. But I most certainly don't. And you know why? Because I take Husker Showers, that's why.

Nebraska was playing the University of Missouri on television, see.

NU was top-ranked but was losing late in the game to a surprisingly difficult bunch of Tigers, and things had just taken a turn for the worse. Mizzou's Brock Olivo had plowed his way for a first down, which meant Nebraska had to get the ball back on the next set of downs or MU could run out the clock and complete the biggest upset of the year.

So I got up and headed for the bathroom. I couldn't bear to watch the Cornhuskers lose; the game was in Columbia, and it was sure to be a screaming, mugging-for-the-camera, tearing-down-of-the-goalposts variety of celebration by throngs of drunken college students. I also decided to take a shower partly because I hadn't taken one yet that day. We'd moved to California earlier that year, and with the time-zone change I hadn't quite gotten a handle on Football Saturdays starting at 9 a.m. I used lots of soap and washed my hair twice and made sure to stay in long enough so the mirror and all the windows fogged over. I got out, put my red clothing back on, and returned to the living room. Kathy was on the couch, reading.

"They've got the ball back," she said matter-of-factly. "But there's only like a minute left."

Sixty-two seconds, to be precise, fifty-five of which the Big Red burned in a last-ditch drive to Missouri's 12-yard line. With no time-outs left, Scott Frost sent two receivers to the left and two to the right for one final shot at the end zone. On what figured to be the game's final play, No. 7 fired the ball hard over the middle to wingback Shevin Wiggins, who caught it for a second before being hit by MU's Julian Jones. The ball trickled down Wiggins's legs, and when he hit the ground his legs popped up – and so did the ball.

As the pigskin floated end-over-end toward the Faurot Field turf, Matt Davison dove in and snuck both hands under it. The officials flung their arms to the sky, Davison leaped to his feet, and the Tiger fans ready to storm the field wandered back to their seats in that stupor Missouri fans are famous for. Within moments, Nebraska completed its remarkable comeback by running past the Tigers in overtime.

Two things happened that day: NU remained unbeaten thanks to one of the most memorable plays in school history and a powerful custom was born. In the years since, I've employed the Husker Shower when it looks like the breaks are going to beat the boys, and it always gives them a boost. I got sudsy later that same season, in fact, to help NU stave off a late Colorado Buffalo run in the thin air out in Boulder. But I am aware of the Husker Shower's power, and I am careful not to abuse it. I reserve it as a last resort, only to be used in the gravest of circumstances so as not to dilute its magical powers.

I realize it's pretty silly to think stripping naked and applying hot water and soap on my body somehow helps the team, especially from great distances. Perhaps it's genetic, though: My mother, too high-strung to watch big games in their entirety, takes naps if the Huskers fall behind, which is sort of the same ritual, minus the water and the Lifebuoy.

My sister Kristy, meanwhile, swears it was her taking off her sweat-shirt in Miami to reveal a tattered old Nebraska T-shirt that powered the Cornhuskers to their Orange Bowl victory over the Hurricanes, not Cory Schlesinger's touchdown runs (or Dave Webber's magic corn cob, the most famous of Husker amulets). My cousin Robbie claims partial responsibility for the win too. He believes it's because he locked one of his friends in his bathroom during the fourth quarter because Nebraska scored every time she went in there to pee.

But I know my family's not the only ones who has game rites. Before each televised game my friend Mindy used to put tiny ceramic figurines of Mr. Roarke and Tattoo from *Fantasy Island* on top of her TV, which I can only assume cast evil spells on the opponent. I know of people who refuse to move from their chair if NU is playing well, or force themselves and others to sit on the floor during crucial points of games. Some people I know fly their Husker flags or windsock from their porch on game day, putting it up and taking it down at the same time each week. Some people believe if they wear all red, they'll charm the Huskers; others believe no red at all works even better. I have one acquaintance who goes into his kitchen a half-hour before a TV game and sets his microwave timer for twenty-five minutes. Then he keeps away from the television until the timer beeps, at which point he turns on the TV just in time to catch the pregame introductions. Mess it up once, and the Big Red is doomed.

My friend Corey and I have often tried to drink the Cornhuskers to victory. They once hit a long bomb for a touchdown as we both polished off our bottles of Fat Tire Ale, and we could've sworn they did the same thing a couple weeks later when we were putting back the exact same stuff. Future attempts at this technique have been sketchy, along with our memories.

When attending games in person, I've noticed NU plays better if I imbibe at the same bars in the same order – first Sandy's, then Barry's, then the N-Zone – before heading over to the grounds. I refuse to meet anyone at the bronze statue in front of Memorial Stadium, because I did that once and the Cornhuskers promptly lost. I attempt to buy my soda and Runza from the same set of vendors at the stadium. And I have my lucky outfit, which I only wear to important games: A faded red hat with its simple white *N* and a gray sweatshirt with "Nebraska" sewed on in shiny scarlet letters. The outfit became an instant tradition after it was unveiled in 1995 against Kansas State, and it ushered the Huskers through twenty-two straight big games with me in the stands. (In all honesty, I am ready to retire the set because it was impotent in Pasadena on January 3, 2002, and several times the following fall.)

None of these has been 100 percent foolproof, though the Husker Showers come close. You hear less about the players' superstitions, though they must certainly have them – wearing particular jersey numbers, growing victory beards, slapping the horseshoe on the way out of the locker room. And theirs are probably more important than ours, especially if they give the athletes the confidence to pick up a blitz or kick the ball straight. They're the ones on the field, after all.

I'd like to think that by combining my game-day spells with theirs, and with those of every red-clad fan in the country, I can somehow make a difference, even though I'm sure in the end they don't mean diddly-squat. But you know what? I can't be absolutely certain of that. So I'm pleased to announce I'll continue to frequent the bars on Football Saturday, while wearing old but comfortable clothes. And when the time comes, at the darkest of hours, I'll do what I have to for my team: I'll take a shower.

Ode to Scott

NEBRASKA 54, TEXAS A&M 15 – DECEMBER 6, 1997

There is a sort of purgatory we fans have for players we have determined, fairly or unfairly, to be failures – guys who, in our expert opinions, were so inept and maligned that their greatest contributions as Cornhuskers was to merely step aside and allow their backups to bring home the glory. The space is crawling with quarter-backs: Mark Mauer lives here for all eternity, as does the last pre-Frazier signal caller, Mike Grant. In this sad realm on the edge of oblivion, these men are all but forgotten. No one cares to drop by, not even for a visit, for fear of being trapped there forever. And once we've passed judgment on an athlete and punched his one-way ticket to this place, there's no way he can escape. Unless he is Scott Frost, that is.

All I know about Scott Frost is what I've read and heard, and that the story – and most people's problems with him – started when he was an all-everything stud at Wood River High, and he made the unthinkable decision to play for Bill Walsh at Stanford instead of doing his patriotic duty and lending his God-given talents to Tom Osborne.

And then Frost came to his senses and transferred to Nebraska two years later but found himself at the scene of the dreaded Lawrence Phillips Incident.

And then Frost didn't, or was unable to, stop Phillips from taking out his frustrations on his former girlfriend, which made more than a few fans think the media blitzkrieg that hit Lincoln was his fault.

And then Frost committed his greatest sin by allowing the infamous crash-and-burn against the Arizona State Sun Devils to occur on his watch, on the same field Tommie Frazier had towered over just nine months earlier no less.

And then we realized that no matter how hard we wished for it, Frost was never going to be Tommie Frazier.

And then when it was clear that he was about as popular in Nebraska as a steakhouse in New Dehli, Frost told reporters he didn't really care what the Joe Six-Packs of the world thought of him, which made him look smug and clueless all at the same time.

And then the jokes started to fly, like the one about Frost and Billy Graham being the only two people on Earth who could make twenty thousand people leap from their seats and yell, "Jesus Christ!"

And then after Frost was underwhelming in a rainy 17-12 home victory over hated Colorado, Tom Osborne made excuses for him, saying Frost had small hands and couldn't hold onto the ball very well when it was wet, which made everyone laugh and wonder why the kid thought he was a Division I–caliber quarterback.

And then my mom, who never said anything bad about anyone

who wore the scarlet and cream, called me on the phone and referred to Frost as "kind of cocky."

And then Frost helped the team to eleven wins, a No. 6 final ranking, and a victory in the Orange Bowl, and since all that didn't involve a Sears Trophy or a call from President Clinton, it wasn't good enough for me, my mom, or anyone else who wore red.

And then before the 1997 season, my friend Michael predicted Frost would be named to the all–Big 12 team at the end of the year, and at the time I suspected something had gone terribly wrong with one of Michael's lab experiments and he had lapsed into the depths of insanity.

And then against Central Florida a few weeks later, Frost jogged back into the huddle after taking a series off, and the stadium realized he was returning to the game and a chorus of boos began to ring out. And then in the locker room after the victory, Frost cried.

And then the following week, there was talk about Frankie London of Louisiana and Bobby Newcombe of New Mexico being better quarterbacks than Frost, if only because they were from states other than Nebraska.

And then the next time the Big Red took the field, against the No. 2 and unbeaten Washington Huskies in Seattle before a national television audience, Frost turned into a human battering ram, blasting for two touchdowns to lead the Cornhuskers to their biggest victory of the young season.

And then sometime after Nebraska mopped the floors with the Huskies, Frost was no longer Frost, but instead known to everyone as Scott.

And then I watched, from my sofa in California, as Scott played virtually flawless football through the incredible autumn of 1997, and I heard how No. 7 jerseys were selling fast down at the Nebraska Bookstore, especially after he ran for the winning score to beat Missouri in overtime.

And then when a reporter suggested to him his running ability was the difference in that Missouri contest, he replied haughtily, "Yeah, it was," and I realized all that separated Scott from being "Frost" again was a fluke catch by a freshman from Tecumseh.

And then Scott kept plowing on, steering Nebraska to yet another undefeated regular season by running over defenders and flinging the football with efficiency and guiding his option pitches into the arms of Ahman Green with telekinetic precision.

And then Scott became just the ninth player in college football history to both run and pass for 1,000 yards in the same year.

And then a few days before the Big 12 Championship Game in San Antonio, Scott was named to the Associated Press All–Big 12 team, as Michael had predicted. However, he was only elected to the second team, behind Missouri's Corby Jones.

And then the coaches voted him on the third team, behind Jones and Kansas State's Michael Bishop, which enraged Husker fans at how little respect their record-setting quarterback was getting around the league.

And then in Nebraska's 54-15 thrashing of Texas A&M in the conference title game, Scott accumulated nearly 300 yards of offense, but his defining play was a block on cornerback Shaun Horn that was so vicious it should have had an R rating, and everyone in red raved about how tough and hard-nosed Scott was.

And then in the weeks before the Orange Bowl showdown with Tennessee, some writer mentioned how Scott was booed earlier in the year, and lots of Husker fans disputed the accuracy of the report, saying that it was just the student section that booed Scott – we would never do that, no way no how.

And then when we flew home from California for Christmas, my brother-in-law Kevin told me he was at that game, sitting across the way from the student section. And to this day he claims with a smile his own section was screaming at Scott, but what they were yelling was "We never doubted yooo-oooo-ooou!"

And now, though it was officially listed as a sellout, no one seems to have even *been* at that Central Florida game – as if it were Woodstock in reverse, or something.

And now when we talk about Scott, he is and always will be Scott, one of the greatest Huskers ever, and he's a world away from guys like Mark Mauer and Mike Grant.

And now when we see Scott around town, we call out his name and wave, and he usually waves back and smiles. But it's sort of a shrewd smile. Because to be one of the greatest Huskers of all time, you have to be flawless. And to be flawless means that we never would have any reason to doubt you. And now, he lets us repeat it, over and over again: You're the best, Scotty Boy. We loved you right from the start.

The Tomfather

NEBRASKA 42, TENNESSEE 17 – JANUARY 2, 1998

I was twenty-six in 1997, but at the time I remember feeling a lot older. Part of it, I'm sure, had to do with my job. Newspapers have an uncanny ability of turning young people into fuddy-duddies long before they're due; sitting in endless zoning commission meetings and working in an office full of hard-faced old grumps will suck your youthful enthusiasm away pretty damn quick. Plus, I was living in California, sixteen hundred miles away from any of my relatives, and so that meant I was also sixteen hundred miles from constantly being reminded that I had come along last in my family. In a way, it was kind of nice being a grown-up, though leaving Circuit City with a washer and dryer instead of the latest PlayStation game took some getting used to.

But when the Huskers came onto the air each week – sometimes on TV, sometimes on a fuzzy radio station out of Glendale – I always felt like a kid again. I would be in a backyard hammock slung between two palm trees, cheering on athletes five, six, even seven years my junior, but in my mind I was twelve years old and at Smith's Standard Station along Highway 77, listening to Lyell Bremser's voice ring out across the state. And the Cornhuskers, they were forever the towering red giants who never faltered, always triumphed, and always led into battle by the great and powerful Tom Osborne.

For all I knew, it was in Osborne's contract that he would coach until the end of time. He was the only person I'd ever seen stalk Nebraska's sidelines, after all, and the idea of anyone else leading the team seemed foreign and illogical. My brain told me it was feasible, of course; I'd heard the stories about him nearly leaving for Colorado in the late '70s, and I remember the calls in the early '90s for him to hang it up for fear we would be doomed to horrible nine-win seasons forever. And in 1997 I'd heard whispers in shadowy corners of the Internet that this season would be his last. So while I conceded it was possible for the Cornhuskers to someday be forced to exist without Tom Osborne, I just never expected someday to come.

Well, it did, with a thunderous boom, on December 10, 1997. I've

heard some Nebraskans compare that day, when Tom Osborne announced his retirement, to the day President Kennedy was shot, at
least in the context of being able to remember exactly where you
were when the news reached you (I was biting into a sourdough ba-
gel at my desk at the newspaper, wondering if the head of the local
zoning board was ever going to return my call). The peaceful, ceremonial transfer of power that elevated Frank Solich to head coach
was similarly presidential, even as it conjured up images of Bob
Devaney hand-picking Osborne himself a quarter-century earlier.
Watching the program's mechanism of succession play out –
Osborne at the podium, flanked by his wife, his players, and Solich –
was like seeing a long-awaited prophecy finally come true. Though
everyone was doing all this for the first time in a generation, they
seemed to know exactly what to do.

Kathy and I flew to Nebraska four days later to start our Christmas
vacation. Already Dr. Tom tribute songs were filling up radio airtime.
Billboards with Osborne's likeness and the words "Thanks, Coach"
were sprouting up. Down at the Nebraska Bookstore – it's every ex-
patriated Nebraskan's duty to stop at the Nebraska Bookstore when
he is home for a visit, lest a curse be put upon his house for all his
days – thousands of patrons had signed a seven-foot, three-sided retirement card with best wishes. I spent a good half-hour reading the
sentiments – "You Rock, T.O.," "We Love You, Man," "Thanks for the
Memories, Tom" – and then picked up the black Magic Marker and
added my own: "Don't do it."

Well, someone had to say what nearly everyone was thinking. It
was simply *too soon* for T.O. to disappear. Big-time football coaches
leave after either overstaying their welcome (think Vince Dooley at
Georgia, Joe Paterno at Penn State) or with their programs in lawless
shambles (think OU's Barry Switzer). Osborne was in neither camp.
He was at the top of his game, and the Nebraska Cornhuskers were
college football's pre-eminent power. The Huskers had outpaced the
rest of the field by embodying Osborne's vision; NU had become a
deliberate, destructive force that blasted opponents into submission
with overwhelming strength and sheer muscle. I didn't want to see
that dominance end. No one did. The Cornhuskers had steamrolled
to a 59-3 record in five years, and in less than a month, they would
travel to the Orange Bowl with yet another national title at stake,

giving Osborne one final opportunity to justify the system he'd spent years perfecting.

Above all, the game in Miami was a last chance to show the nation the way we did things in Nebraska, and for our money there was no one better than Tom Osborne to show them. It goes without saying that long before he even considered becoming a Congressman, Osborne was the face of our state to the rest of the country. He was white, one-hunnert-and-ten-percent Republican, a devout Christian, an avid outdoorsman. He was an unassuming, private, simple man who didn't drink, smoke, or use profanity. He lived his life in a straight line and found comfort in his routines and his processes. Who better to represent all of us ordinary Nebraska folks, with our workaday, blue-collar lives, doing business with a handshake and a smile? Bob Kerrey? Ben Nelson? Mike Johanns? Puh-leease.

Osborne's persona so dominated the state, in fact, that it was not a stretch for us to believe a sporting event predicated on simulated warfare and physical violence could have some kind of religious message. Here was a guy who won eight of every ten football games he coached but constantly carped about it not being about wins and losses. It was about honoring God, you see. It was more than winning. It was a masterful credo, one that gave a righteous purpose and meaning to Football Saturday while inoculating Osborne from criticism after a rare defeat. *Yeah, we lost to Oklahoma today, but hey, have you heard the Good News? Success can't be determined by wins or losses, it's a whole lot bigger than that, and besides, we're still going to the Citrus Bowl.* It was a spectacular salve the Sunday after a particularly stinging loss. Still, we never really got to test how many of us actually drank the Kool-Aid. After all, Osborne never went .500, never had a team that didn't make it to a good bowl game, and never finished outside the Top 25. If he had, the assumption was that we fans would accept our fortunes with dignity and grace, give thanks for having such wonderful kids on the team, and proclaim that the loss was all part of some divine plan.

In '97 Lee Corso called Nebraska "God's team," in reference to Matt Davison's lucky catch against Missouri. He meant it as a joke, but we didn't really get it. How could we? The football-as-ministry doctrine struck a sharp chord with the most devout among us, that group who heard "Onward Christian Soldiers" when the band played "Hail Varsity." To them the sinful opponents, representing amoral Sodom-lands like California, Florida, or Colorado, were deserving of good floggings. And then, when the heathens were sufficiently flayed, Os-borne administered the last rites, telling reporters the contest was a lot closer than the dadgum scoreboard indicated. He'd do it in that aw-shucks tone of his, but if you looked closely, you'd see that know-ing twinkle in his eye.

That was another thing that made Tom Osborne the Nebraskanest Nebraskan of all. Behind his simpleton veneer we suspected there was a cold, calculating, streetwise, politically savvy operator who knew precisely what the score was and knew exactly what buttons to press to get what he needed. His wry smile after the Huskers deci-mated Florida in the Fiesta Bowl was the same one my dad used to get when someone from New York or L.A. would come rolling in-to Smith's Standard Station for gas, notice that a large puddle of antifreeze was forming under his BMW, and then ask my dad if he thought that was anything to worry about.

I'm not a very religious person, so in my adult life I've struggled with the saints-vs.-sinners approach to Husker fandom. But it's prob-ably no coincidence that I compare Tom Osborne to my dad. You figure there are a few routes to sports fandom when you're a kid: 1) geographic ties to a particular team; 2) latching onto a good team because everyone else does; and 3) your dad likes a certain team. It's why I still suffer through long hot summers of Kansas City Royals "baseball," and why on fall Sundays I watch the Minnesota Vikings find marvelous new ways to fall flat on their faces. Those are my dad's teams too. Tom Osborne is my father's age, and sometimes when he says words like *Missourah* and *wudn't* and *warsh*, he sounds just like my dad. So to me, our coach wasn't a Father Tom, but more like a father, Tom.

Nebraska's opponent in the 1998 Orange Bowl, the No. 3 Tennessee Volunteers, probably wouldn't have minded if Osborne had handed the keys off to Solich one game early. The Volunteers were the best squad in the best league that year, the Southeastern Conference, but came into the game as 17-point underdogs to the Big Red. There was, however, a much bigger adversary on January 2: the polls. The Corn-huskers were ranked second behind Michigan and needed to pro-duce a decisive victory in Miami if they had any hope of splitting the national title with the Wolverines. Fittingly, for Osborne's final team, it was going to come down to "more than winning" in a literal sense. To get the blowout the Huskers were looking for they had to rattle UT's all-everything quarterback, Peyton Manning. They had to pound Tennessee's defense to the ground and control time of possession. They needed to play with resolve and spirit and precision. They needed an Osborne Classic.

They got it. Leading 14-3, Nebraska took the second-half kickoff and drove 80 yards in the most Osborne-like manner possible. Ahman Green carried seven times, Scott Frost three, and Joel Makovicka and Bobby Newcombe once each in a twelve-play drive that featured no passing and ended with Frost keeping the ball for 6 points. On Tennessee's next offensive series, the Vols were crushed for minimal gain on two straight running plays, forcing Manning to throw on third down. But defensive end Mike Rucker knifed into the Volunteer backfield and whacked him to the turf. The Volunteers were through.

The Huskers kept hammering away – Frost off-tackle, Green on the delay, Makovicka up the middle – until the Pro Player Stadium scoreboard read Nebraska 42, Tennessee 17. When the final second of his final game had ticked away, Osborne accepted the Bowl Alliance trophy, handshakes from the Orange Bowl committee, and congratulations from CBS's Michelle Tafoya, then jogged off the field nonchalantly, as if he'd just racked up another win against Baylor. As he disappeared into the stadium tunnel, I thought about how many times he had come to this place, this city, this bowl game, and had left on the short end of a heartbreaking defeat. But that was an old story now. Tom Osborne had beaten the Orange Bowl a few years earlier; now, he'd simply mastered it. Later that night, Nebraska won the coaches' poll.

In the following days and weeks, I put my charge card to the test, snatching up all the commemorative merchandise I could find – newspapers, HuskerVision videos, game tapes, special pullout sections from the *Omaha World-Herald* and the *Lincoln Journal Star*. But all the tributes in the world couldn't really convince me that it was time for this era to end.

I didn't really feel it until the following August, when Frank Solich coached his first game against Louisiana Tech in Lincoln. Nebraska was ahead 14-0, and the cameras cut to a close-up of Bobby Newcombe, and it hit me. He looked young, really young. So did all of his teammates, in fact – even the ones like Kris Brown and Mike Rucker, who had played most of their careers for Osborne.

I realized then, for the first time, that with every year that passed I would identify with the players less and less, and the older I got the stranger it would feel wearing the replica jersey of a twenty-one year old. I stood at the edge of a gap that I knew would only grow wider: I would grow older each year, but they would stay the same age, and then they'd be gone – along with Tom Osborne, who had prolonged my childhood for more than a decade. Every week Dr. Tom told me stories that almost always had a happy ending, and if they didn't, well, I still had someone to tuck me in at night, to tell me it was part of something bigger and that it was going to be all right.

I looked around the screen. Everything seemed to be in place: The fans were in red, the signs were hanging along the stadium walls, the band was playing the school song, the Cornhuskers were well ahead on the scoreboard. It was exactly like every other Football Saturday, except for one big difference: I didn't feel like a kid any more.

Big Red Country

NEBRASKA 41, KANSAS STATE 15 - NOVEMBER 13, 1999

If I had to choose between moving and having to watch the Kansas State Wildcats win the Big 12 title, I might just consider the latter. Studies have shown that, aside from enduring the death of a loved one, getting divorced, or losing your job, the biggest emotional hamburger drill you can put yourself through is picking up your life and depositing it in a new city. It's not fun, it's a lot of hard work, and you're bombarded with uncertainty day and night. On the bright side, you do get to eat at a lot of fast-food establishments along the way.

In October 1999 an odd turn of events sent Kathy and me packing for Reno, Nevada. This would be our fourth big move in six years. Since graduating from college we'd spent three years in Iowa City, a year and a half in central California, and two more down south near Los Angeles. Now the itinerary pointed north.

Native Nevadans, all six of them, will tell you Reno is a pretty nice town. It's along the Truckee River and at the foot of the stunning Sierra Nevada, and its high-desert climes bring weather in moderate slices. Lake Tahoe and world-class skiing bring tourists in droves, too, and give Reno its title of Biggest Little City in the World, though oddly, it's only the third-largest city in Nevada.

However, if you're a clumsy flatlander like me who can't ski and prefers to acquire goods and services with his paycheck instead of doubling down on 11, the place doesn't have a lot to offer. And unlike the hustle-and-bustle urbanity of Southern California, where the towns and cities meld into one another, Reno is isolated from other population centers. It's seven hours to Vegas, three to San Francisco, and a full day's drive to Salt Lake City. It might as well be on the moon, and that's not much of a stretch – five steps outside of the town's neon glow, the landscape looks like something out of an Apollo mission.

Having become experts of sorts in relocating, we figured we'd settle into our new city with relative ease. But Reno was unlike any town we'd ever moved to. Every place was open 24/7. There were rows of slot machines in the gas stations, grocery stores, and Laundromats. The best places to eat were in casinos, which all smelled of cigarette smoke and carpet glue and were filled with shriveled gamblers who looked like they hadn't moved from their stools since Bush Sr. was president. Most people looked desperate, disheveled, debauched, or a combination of the three.

Determined to make the best of it, Kathy and I pulled into our new home a few days ahead of the moving truck. It had been delayed, which in Moving Truck Standard Time meant "right on schedule." But we didn't expect the house to seem as bare as it did. We spread out the belongings we'd brought with us – the computer, a small color TV, and an inflatable mattress to sleep on – but that didn't help much.

The Friday before we started work, a ray of normalcy arrived: We got our first piece of mail. It was from our new boss, a Kansas graduate. Inside was a newspaper clipping that read:

NORTHERN NEVADANS FOR NEBRASKA
*A supporters group for fans, friends, and alumni of the University of Nebraska
Weekly Game Watch Parties at the Pinon Plaza Casino and Hotel, Carson City
Come join the fun!*

I'd been to only one other "supporters group" gathering before, a Californians for Nebraska meet-up in Hermosa Beach to watch the Cornhuskers puree an overmatched patsy on some bar's satellite TV.

It was me and a couple of large, blank-faced men who didn't speak at all. I wasn't warm to the idea of driving thirty miles into the Nevada desert for an encore of that. By the same token, I wouldn't want to be around too many people, because then I'd be expected to socialize, an activity at which I am notoriously awful when NU is on the tube. On Football Saturdays, I don't want to talk about the news, politics, my job, someone else's job, or anything else resembling normal conversation. In fact, I'm *incapable* of it. So the only choice was to watch Nebraska's upcoming showdown with Kansas State on my tiny Toshiba in the empty living room.

"Yeah, well, the game isn't on the local ABC station out here tomorrow," Kathy said. "So I guess you won't be watching it at all."

OK, so Carson City it was. Luckily, we'd brought a couple of Husker shirts with us, so when we pulled into the casino parking lot we could be identified as friendlies. And it's good we got there early because the Pinon Plaza was packed. There must've been seventy people dressed in red in the joint's party room, all of them orbiting around a giant-screen TV tuned to ABC's pregame analysis. The waitresses were even wearing Eric Crouch jerseys – nice touch. It was like someone had transported Barry's Bar to the middle of the high desert.

I'd heard about these gatherings, where Husker fans come out of the woodwork on Game Day whether they're in York, Nebraska, or York, Pennsylvania. The nation is peppered with area safe houses – Capital of Texas Nebraskans, Southern Arizonans for Nebraska, Kentuckiana Huskers, the Oklahoma Cornhusker Club – and in the years before ESPN GamePlan, these red enclaves would stop at nothing on Football Saturdays to make their respective area codes feel a little bit more like 402. Some friends in California talked of Bay Area Husker groups that would get Valentino's and Runzas FedEx-ed in just in time for kickoff, while my oldest sister, Kim, and her husband, Jeff, used to host Georgians for Nebraska "earwitness" parties. Jeff would call a relative in Nebraska, who would set her receiver next to KFAB's broadcast of the game, and Jeff would put his phone on speaker. Dozens of uprooted Husker fans would gather around each week to listen.

All that was before the Internet and satellite TV, which could bring the Huskers into anyone's living room. I figured that access would end, or at least thin out, many of the gatherings. But here in northern Nevada, the Husker community was alive and well: Amicable red-clad people mingled about, laughing and chatting like they were old friends. It was strangely inviting; there was not a familiar face in the whole room, but at the same time I'd seen every one of these folks before.

Upon seeing us enter, a jolly fellow named Lanny Lemburg, who originally hailed from Dannebrog, ambled over and asked me where I was from. When I told him, he immediately said, "Rosalie! Dick Gustin!" And I knew right then Lanny had to be an antiques buff, because Dick Gustin, who lived up the street when I was a kid, has an antiques dealership known far and wide. This happens all the time when Nebraskans get together. It's like our version of the Six Degrees to Kevin Bacon game. Everyone either knows you or knows someone who does.

It wasn't a particularly football-savvy crowd. There were some hardcore fans at the Pinon Plaza, sure, but overall, the event felt like a small-town alumni banquet. The clash between NU and KSU appeared to be the reason to gather but soon became so much background noise. Maybe if I lived away longer, or if I wasn't so hopelessly obsessed with the team's fortunes, I would fully understand this perspective, which suggests it's the existence of the game that's important and not so much whether a Bowl Championship Series bid is on the line. To many there, it really was only a game, and it probably was good for me to hang out with people who viewed football as nothing more than a distraction, though at the time I thought they had their priorities completely out of whack because a bcs bowl *was* on the line that day.

To that point Nebraska's season had been more like *Days of Our Huskers*. Bobby Newcombe started the year as the No. 1 quarterback, though Crouch had clearly been outplaying him. Frustrated, Crouch went AWOL, which sent Head Coach Frank Solich chasing him to Millard. When Crouch returned, Newcombe magically switched to wingback. Meanwhile, I-back DeAngelo Evans quit after failing to convince Solich the ball needed to be in his hands every play. Sometime during all of this, running back Correll Buckhalter also disappeared for a few days and was assumed to be off the team. Then, when things seemed to be settling down, NU lost to goddamned Texas and fell into a mid-season funk. They barely beat Kansas – *Kansas!* – and then fooled around against Texas A&M before eventually pulling away for a win.

K-State, meanwhile, was ranked fifth nationally. The Wildcats, who hadn't been touched through nine games in '99, were the defending division champs and had a vaunted defensive unit. But Nebraska, behind Crouch and an unsolvable Blackshirt defense, controlled the game throughout. Crouch set the tone on NU's first scoring drive by *becoming* the drive – the Cornhuskers took over the ball at the Wildcat 44, and he ran twice for 14 yards before uncorking a 30-yard touchdown run. NU led by two scores at halftime, then systematically broke Kansas State down in the second half to register a spirited 41-15 victory.

Nebraska's final touchdown came from freshman I-back Dahrran Diedrick, who wore No. 30. Early in the fourth quarter, Diedrick slipped into the secondary, outran everyone in a silver helmet, and tiptoed across the goal line to cap a sweet 46-yard touchdown run. An elderly woman sitting two tables down yelled, "Hey, that's the way to go, Ahman!" I thought about correcting her, but it felt too good to see a running back wearing No. 30 scooting down the sideline again, as did having a quarterback dressed in No. 7 and a defensive end sporting No. 57 with the name KELSAY on the back. In the 1990s Nebraska mastered assembly-line football, reproducing great players and their corresponding jersey numbers like an all-night Kinkos: Defensive tackles wore No. 55, wingbacks No. 33, defensive ends No. 98. The touch was subtle but had to be demoralizing to opponents from year to year: *Yeah, Ahman Green left early, but don't worry, we're gonna stick in another kid just like 'im.*

As the game ended, we got up and bid farewell to the others. On our way out, Kathy and I became card-carrying members of Northern Nevadans for Nebraska. Over the next two years, we were active in the organization, helping plan summer picnics and arranging football watch parties. We did it partly because we were proud alumni and wanted to see a Nebraska-based group flourish in northern Nevada. But mainly we did it because we made some good friends the day the Big Red waxed Kansas State, just three days into our lives as Nevadans, and we owed them all a lot for making us feel right at home.

Parity Poopers

It is widely alleged, in places like Lawrence and Boulder and Columbia and Stillwater and other shantytowns where red makes people angry, that the Nebraska Cornhuskers cheat to win. As the legend goes, all ninety-three counties in Nebraska give out something called "county scholarships" to local football players each year, so the young lads can suit up for the Big Red and save the university some money. Supposedly, these awards don't count toward the NCAA's eighty-five-scholarship limit for Division 1-A universities. That means NU's coaches have more scholarships to work with, see, and that means they can offer more free rides to out-of-state blue-chippers than their rivals can. And that means they get all the good players and win all the time.

This is, of course, bullshit. County scholarships don't exist and never have. If they did, they would qualify as an "extra benefit," which is a giant no-no in the eyes of the NCAA. They enforce this rule pretty stringently: Before the 2000 season, the group slapped Husker quarterback Eric Crouch for eating a complimentary ham sandwich, for Christ's sake. Something tells me if NU was harboring a multimillion-dollar scholarship slush fund, the suits at the NCAA would probably catch wise. But without fail, the myth returns every autumn to rationalize why the Cornhuskers just hung 70 points on Gallbladder State Tech.

Actually, Nebraska sustained its dynasty for four decades by playing to its strengths. Coaches capitalized on the state's border-to-border Big Red mania by attracting walk-on athletes in droves. Meanwhile, NU's offensive philosophy helped convince athletes who otherwise might have sat the bench at a pass-happy university that they would flourish with the Big Red. Boyd Epley's strength and conditioning program also was light years ahead of the field. And it didn't hurt to have the iconic Tom Osborne leading the effort, a core group of longtime, loyal assistants in tow. With a little hunger, drive, and luck, a bevy of national championship commemorative T-shirts followed. This all came during a time when high-profile coaches around the country were grousing about parity, citing the eighty-five-scholarship limit as killer of the status quo: Traditional powers such as Notre Dame, USC, Penn State, and Oklahoma started going through down cycles in the 1990s, while lightweights like Boise State, Virginia Tech, and Oregon State morphed from minnows into sharks.

We Nebraska fans accepted this as even more irrefutable evidence that our program was different and special. In our minds, scholarship reductions were everyone else's problem. Why worry? From 1978 (when the first major reductions occurred and the NCAA placed a cap of ninety-five per school) to 1999 (five years after they were whittled to eighty-five), the Cornhuskers won 84 percent of the time, amassing a 231-41-1 record. To our untrained eyes, not even Osborne's retirement seemed to slow things down. In two seasons, Frank Solich had won a Big 12 championship and the Fiesta Bowl. This was how it should be. After all, the playbook was the same, the style of football was the same, most of the coaching staff was the same. We expected to dominate the Big 12 exactly as we did the Big 8; to suffer USC's or Notre Dame's fate was as unacceptable as it was inconceivable.

But the planets couldn't stay aligned forever. After the Fiesta Bowl win, the heart of the Blackshirts, Charlie McBride, hung up his whistle. Meantime, other schools were catching up – or had already caught up – with Nebraska in the strength and conditioning department. The walk-on program still infused role players into the Husker depth chart, but the cracks were starting to show; schools like Kansas State were sneaking across the state lines, offering scholarships to kids who normally would come to Lincoln and play for free.

Arguably the most damaging blow, however, came in 1996 when the Big 8 became the Big 12. The new conference adopted academic eligibility requirements for incoming student-athletes that were much more restrictive than before. The conference limited member schools in the number of "partial qualifiers" and "non-qualifiers" – code words for student-athletes who came up short on entrance requirements – each year. This was a huge change; before '96, Nebraska would take around a half-dozen a year. It was an often-overlooked contributor to their success. The limits threatened to put Nebraska at a recruiting disadvantage.

None of this had fully taken shape early in Solich's tenure. As far as we knew, Fearless Frankie had deftly kept the Devaney-Osborne lineage intact and all was well. From the looks of his play calling, Nebraska's steamrolling of Tennessee after the 1999 season could have just as easily taken place in '65, '75, '85, or '95. After all the bowls were played that year, many pundits argued Solich's Cornhuskers were the nation's best, and in 2000 the Big Red was No. 1 in both major preseason polls.

But something seemed out of kilter from the start. NU needed overtime to beat No. 23 Notre Dame in South Bend and looked uninspired in wins over Iowa, Missouri, and Iowa State. The team seemed to hit stride with detonations of Texas Tech and Baylor but then was crushed by the resurgent Oklahoma Sooners in a 1-vs.-2 showdown in Norman in the Game of the Century III or IV or V or whatever number they were on by then. Two weeks later NU suffered a 1-point road loss to Kansas State, then needed a walk-off field goal to beat 3-8 Colorado in Lincoln. The same day Oklahoma accepted an invitation to the national title game in Miami, the Cornhuskers, who three and a half months earlier were everyone's front-runners for the Orange Bowl, politely nodded when the Sylvania Alamo Bowl summoned them to San Antonio. For the second time in three years, NU would be part of ESPN's Thrifty Rental Bowl Week. Ick.

To claim that a year-end trip to the Alamodome was every Cornhusker fan's dream would be an insult. The cagey adversary, the Northwestern Wildcats, were a perfect symbol of the state of the game – one of the losingest teams of the last one hundred years, they'd gone from being everyone's homecoming opponent to co-conference champion. And they hailed from the Big 10, the poster-league for uniformity and balance, where an 8-3 record can get you a trophy and a nifty championship ring. No one from Evanston thought the 2000 season had been a failure, that's for sure. And knocking off Nebraska, even a tottering Nebraska, would make the Wildcats' year, if not their century.

Like most old-money Husker fans, I was offended by this turn of events. In one moment of asinine crankiness, I declared I'd rather blow the family nest egg at the Flamingo Hilton in Reno than watch the Alamo Bowl on TV. It was a nothing game against a nobody opponent with nothing at stake. The only way it would be memorable was if Northwestern were to win, and then the Wildcats could add it to their list of greatest wins in school history. Which, soberly enough, was possible: The Wildcats had one of those cunning offenses that spread the field and fashioned big plays, the kind of attack Craig Bohl's Blackshirts had struggled with all year. However, my worry didn't last long: On the Huskers' first drive of the second quarter, Crouch ripped off one of his patented so-long-farewell touchdown gallops, and it became clear Nebraska had solved Northwestern. The offensive line was pushing the Wildcats back five yards, and the old-fashioned butt-kicking was on.

It was like watching men against boys; it really was. In the third quarter, with NU up 52-17, Crouch wheeled to his right and tossed the ball to Bobby Newcombe, 5 yards behind the line of scrimmage. Newcombe then released a rainbow toward No. 3, Matt Davison, who was running wide open downfield. Davison caught the ball, jogged in for the score, ran to the center of the end zone and flung both hands to the sky.

Those in purple booed, alleging the Cornhuskers were running it up. And they probably were. Besides, who can argue with Northwestern fans? They're so used to watching their team get bludgeoned, after all, they came up with the cheer "That's all right, that's ok, you'll all work for us some day." And they're supposedly really smart, so they must know the subtle differences between a classy, sportsman-like rout and a mean, vindictive rout. Not that it mattered; they were all heading for the exits anyway.

Husker fans, of course, stayed until the very end. Who could blame any of us for wanting it to go on forever? The veteran leaders on this squad were just freshmen when Dr. Tom coached his last down, and as the final seconds faded away in San Antonio, so did the last vestiges of the Osborne era. Appropriately enough, it ended with the crushing of an undermanned opponent.

The stands were full of Nebraskans, making the Alamo Bowl feel like a home game. And maybe, I thought as I watched Russ Hochstein raise the trophy, that's where the Cornhuskers get their "extra benefit" – not from the absurd county scholarships but from our unwavering loyalty, energy, and focus. With the playing field more level than ever, I thought, the game's intangibles – coaching, injuries, and most importantly, emotion – meant more than they ever had before. Maybe, just maybe, our demands for excellence would be enough to stave off parity and keep the Huskers defying gravity forever. In the wake of a timeless Nebraska tromping of a college football flunky, it wasn't hard to fool myself into believing this.

I was still in this mindset three weeks later when my telephone rang. It was someone in Lincoln, asking if I was interested in a job there. At first I hesitated, but then I thought about my family and the friends I'd left behind and barbecues with them on humid summer nights. I thought about sugar cones from the UNL Dairy Store, live music at Duffy's, and the weather being the top story on the ten o'clock news. I thought about what it would be like to be unsurprised by someone wearing Husker gear at the supermarket. I thought about pre-gaming at Barry's, about hearing the "Pride of All Nebraska." I thought about walking through the turnstiles, surrounded by red, and climbing up to my seat. I thought about a Nebraska fullback lowering the boom on an unsuspecting linebacker. I thought about Football Saturday and how long it had been since I'd been a real part of it.

And, I thought, maybe it was time to go home.

Home

The Good Life

Nothing makes you feel more like a Cornhusker than to live in places where not everyone is a Cornhusker. For nearly a decade and living in three different states, I never stopped thinking of Nebraska as home, and this is how I was described and identified by those who knew me. As we prepared to leave Reno for Lincoln, however, a co-worker said I'd probably be surprised at how western I'd become. Like what? I asked. The fact I now called pop "soda"? Or that I'd learned to place the word "the" in front of interstates and highways, like "the 80," or "the 395"? He smiled and said, "Oh, you'll see," and left it at that.

Coming back to your homeland after years away provides you with a steady stream of Rip Van Winkle moments. For me they started the first time I drove along Twenty-seventh Street. A gaggle of chain eateries, hotels, and big-box retailers had sprouted up north of Cornhusker Highway. Farther south, past Highway 2, tract housing stretched for acres, and a new shopping center, SouthPointe Pavilions, had been built. Time had wrought changes on campus too: The Nebraska Union was bigger and more modern, along with Broyhill Fountain. Just north, an expansive green space had replaced the gray and gritty faculty parking area I used to cut through on my way to class. The nearly comatose Haymarket District was now booming with clever little shops and a variety of restaurants. Over by the North Bottoms neighborhood, the shine was still on a new $30 million baseball stadium. And for some reason, Lincoln's mayor, Mike Johanns, had moved into the governor's mansion.

But once these revelations became fewer and farther between and Kathy and I settled into our everyday routines, it became evident the enduring images of Lincoln we'd kept through the years were mostly romantic notions. Part of the problem was we left Nebraska immediately after college; requirements of adulthood like getting up before 10:30, paying mortgages, and working full time had never been part of our Star City encounter. To us Lincoln had always been Playland – it was where we'd met, fallen in love, partied with friends, and ate out

135

a lot. But now we were back, all grown up, and the place was different, like a bad sequel to a good movie.

Through that first summer back, I began to recall my Reno co-worker's warning. I'm not sure what made me feel more foreign at Wendy's during a busy lunch hour – the fact that a woman in line in front of me spent three minutes writing a personal check for her $3.29 meal or that no one else thought it was odd. At stoplights I wondered what exactly was going through the guy in the lead car's mind as he sat idle for a full five seconds after the signal turned green. I was weirded out when walking into a local bar or restaurant to realize people at nearly every table would look up, for a really long time, to see who had just entered. It hit me every time I encountered Nebraska's ubiquitous culture of Redneck Cool – women named Melanoma with bad perms and bad dye-jobs in acid-washed jeans; men with goatees and greasy mullets wearing Oakley Blades; pickup trucks with a window sticker of the Calvin and Hobbes kid pissing on the Ford symbol and a pit bull in the back; radio stations playing way too much Sammy Hagar. Most of all I knew we were in Nebraska when we saw no one else our age without children. The only other Lincolnites without a pack of toddlers hanging on them were teenagers and senior citizens. And sometimes they were lugging kids around too. It was bizarre, simultaneously feeling like a fish out of water and perfectly at home. It took some getting used to.

And I won't lie: Nebraska can be pretty suffocating at times. It's homogenous and hyper-reactionary and fairly myopic, and by that I mean more than the lack of an authentic Mexican restaurant in downtown Lincoln. Often you sense the prevailing majority wishes it were still 1954 but not in that Disneyland's-Main-Street-America, tribute-to-a-way-of-life-that-never-really-existed sort of way. Over time this breeds a cynical and bitter sort of citizen who is suspicious of outsiders, resistant to change, and who shuns those who aren't "normal." Then politicians and state officials call a press conference to wonder why hordes of young adults are leaving the state.

All this may make Nebraska sound like a pretty crappy place to live. It's really not. By and large, the people are friendly, store clerks still thank you for your business, and usually the biggest crisis on your street is when two people volunteer at the same time to host this year's Fourth of July party. Then there's the university and everything it brings to the table: stately and venerable buildings, a theater to show films with subtitles, large bookstores, and a texture-filled catchment area around campus made up of bars, pizzerias, record shops, and tattoo parlors.

In the late summer of 2001 I found a great deal of serenity pulling into work and looking up at the big red *N*s on Memorial Stadium's west façade, then walking a block south and hearing the Cornhusker marching band's drum line practicing their game-day routine over on campus. The next lot over stood a weathered sign that read, "Game Day Parking $10." Already the town was gearing up for the Big Red's opener against Texas Christian University.

Before the 2001 season the last college football game I'd been to was in Reno during a Husker off week, where I witnessed an epic WAC confrontation between the Nevada Wolf Pack and the Rice Owls. Seeing how it was late November and the two teams had three wins between them, there was ample seating for anyone willing to part with fourteen dollars for a ticket. That afternoon was some of the most fun I've had at a football game, in an anthropological sense, anyway. I'd often wanted to attend a sporting event where I had no life-or-death stake in the outcome, just to see whether my game-day tendencies came from the game itself or whether they were from the presence of the Cornhuskers. For want of a better term to describe my experience, I was entertained. Nevada won 34-28 in a back-and-forth contest, and the fans in my section literally stood and yelled the whole time. The Wolf Pack left the field to raucous applause, and everyone went home happy. No one seemed too concerned about the next year, or hell, even the next week. It was a nice way to spend a Saturday afternoon, nothing more and nothing less.

By late August I was ready for some big-time college football. Part of me truly believed divine providence had whisked me back to Lincoln just in time for a Husker schedule featuring eight home games, one that also summoned Notre Dame, Oklahoma, and Kansas State to Lincoln. This seemed to be a good omen, so I snagged two tickets in the north end zone for the first game and brought my coworker Larry along.

As we approached the stadium, however, I began to get uncomfortable, and by the time Larry found a stadium seat to rent, I was having a mild anxiety attack. What if all this, too, had been a romantic illusion for all those years? For so long in my time away, I pictured Memorial Stadium as the one place where I unquestionably *belonged.*

Would that ideal be shattered? Would Football Saturday be strangely alien, too, in that sad, disconnected way I had come to feel about much of Nebraska?

I staved off panic by realizing that dwelling on such notions would inevitably make them come true, much in the same way that the very act of observation changes that which is being observed. So I put it out of my mind as best I could – which wasn't easy. Instead of its traditional white uniforms, the band marched in red polo shirts and khaki shorts. Then a flyover that was supposed to punctuate the national anthem interrupted it instead. The Tunnel Walk animation was predictably schmaltzy, and HuskerVision continually told us to turn our attention toward it. Rough start.

The Huskers had no such problem. On their fourth play from scrimmage, Eric Crouch navigated through the Horned Frog defense for 33 exhilarating yards, and Thunder Collins ran for 12 more to the TCU 6. Then Collins blasted across for a score, the place went bonkers, and all was forgotten. The Huskers, who were a huge favorite of the oddsmakers, looked like they were going to dispatch Texas Christian with the greatest of ease. But moments later, Frog quarterback Casey Printers threw a 67-yard touchdown pass, and Memorial Stadium grew silent.

Well, almost silent. Though the Cornhuskers answered quickly with another touchdown and led 13-7, the mood in the stands was uncomfortable at best. Crouch was sacked three times and intercepted in the second quarter as Texas Christian ratcheted up the pressure. When the teams headed to the locker rooms, a small throng of purple-clad fans put Memorial Stadium to shame by loudly chanting, "T-C-U! T-C-U!"

It was sometime around this point when I first encountered the Shrill Woman Up and To My Left. Everyone knows this woman, bedecked in a white sun visor and bad sunglasses and with a voice that can peel paint off the walls. On this particular Football Saturday, she efficiently rotated between one of two exclamations: During a play, she would belt out an indignant "Come ON!" and then if the result was not to her satisfaction, she would follow up with a "You STUPID IDIOTS!" The Shrill Woman Up and To My Left is still around to this day; she is always there, wearing her sun visor and bad sunglasses no matter what Big Red sporting event I'm at.

Everyone else was in a bad mood too, even as Crouch tore off another long run, the Huskers marched 98 yards in the third quarter for a score, and the Blackshirts clamped down to seal the victory. The final was 21-7, but already people were talking about how the Cornhuskers couldn't pick up a blitz to save their lives and how badly Notre Dame would've whomped them had they been in Lincoln that day. Others were doing fan math, that subjective arithmetic where a guy can determine what the final score might have been if it weren't for a couple of key plays. Fan math had declared the Pigskin Classic a 7-7 tie.

With a few minutes left and Nebraska's offense milking the clock and in no hurry to score, a large, goateed man in front of Larry and me stood, loudly proclaimed he'd seen enough garbage for one day, and headed for the exit.

Jesus, it was good to be back.

Flag Football

NEBRASKA 48, RICE 3 – SEPTEMBER 20, 2001

The ball was at the Rice 42 as Eric Crouch brought the Cornhuskers to the line of scrimmage. Then No. 7 took the snap, pivoted to his right, and feigned putting the ball into Thunder Collins's belly. Instead, Crouch took three steps toward the west sideline, reared back, and flung the ball high toward the end zone. Downfield, a sprinting Wilson Thomas had beaten his man. He looked up, planted his feet, and leaped. Extending every inch of his 6-foot-6 frame, Thomas snagged the pass, pulled it to his chest, and came to earth amid colored turf. The official flung his arms skyward, signaling touchdown, and we rose from our seats and roared. Nebraska was going to win the ballgame, and win big.

Suffice it to say the Cornhuskers have long been the id of the state of Nebraska – as the team goes, so goes the rest of the state. As such, there's nothing better for our collective peace of mind than when the Huskers smother their prey early, a record or two gets broken, and the Big Red's huddle is bursting with fourth- and fifth-stringers by the end of the game. That way, we know the sun is shining, God is in his heaven, and all is right in the universe. On September 20, 2001, Nebraska socked the Rice Owls with 21 first-quarter points, Crouch became the all-time Big 12 quarterback rushing leader, and when the gun sounded they were pulling guys out of the stands to play line-backer. Nine days after September 11, this was just what we needed.

Like everyone else, I was scared and confused and angry and still in shock. I'd spent way too much time over the past week watching CNN and staring at my palms. I wondered, along with many others, how much of a crowd would show up to watch Nebraska-Rice, the first major college football game to be played after the attacks. As it turned out, we filled the place, if for no other reason than it seemed to be the normal thing to do.

But as with everything else, "normal" was suddenly a relative term. What exactly did that mean now? Even here, in our sanctuary, were constant reminders of the dire happenings in New York and Washington DC. Where soda vendors usually stood, Red Cross workers pleaded for donations to help the victims. Up on the big screens, Tom Osborne tried in his calmest voice to comfort us, but we knew even he didn't have any answers. Fans still clung to their portable radios, but it was to hear the president's address to Congress, not Warren Swain's account of the action down below. And the American flag over the east stands was a mammoth creation – thirty-five yards long, at least, and big enough for all 77,344 of us to wrap ourselves in.

Yes, between the "U-S-A" chants, the Tunnel Walk honoring our public servants, and a video montage of the rescue efforts set to the music of Ray Charles, a vigorous measure of American pride was at work. And that undoubtedly helped us allow ourselves to cheer again. The stadium was uproariously loud, as deafening as I can remember, as the game started; Rice's first possession started inside its own 10-yard line and promptly went backward thanks to the clamor. I joined in the chorus of noisemakers from the south stands in hopes of discombobulating the Owls' quarterback, who was clearly struggling to get his cadence heard. But even as I did, I felt guilty – that I was yelling against another American; that I didn't give more money to the donation takers out front; that I was even here in the first place, braying for blood, while at Ground Zero the mayor was requesting a thousand more body bags. For the first time, Memorial Stadium was not the center of the universe. And like most of the other revelations from that awful autumn, it was sobering and surreal.

Until that point, I unashamedly used the Nebraska Cornhuskers as my lens to the world. I continually introduced badly chosen football metaphors into conversations about religion, politics, or social issues and staved off scoffs by reminding my friends that sports didn't exist in a vacuum. The heavy topics in the Op-Ed section, I argued, weren't mutually exclusive from the ones on the sports page, so football was an ample allegory for life. At thirty years of age, I thought I had things all figured out. However, if September 11 taught me anything, it was that I really didn't have a clue. The illusion was gone; my hard-headed, football-is-life vision of the world was too archaic, too inflexible, too goddamned *simple* to help me understand a very complicated world.

Within weeks, explosions rocked Afghanistan as the so-called War on Terror began. But war is hell to comprehend, so most people find it easier to simplify the world into sharp contrasts – just like in football. When the bombs began to strike Kabul, online Husker bulletin boards broke into a collective patriotic pep rally, featuring messages like "Go Big Red, White, and Blue," and "U.S. 77, Taliban 3," and "G.B.R. and G.B.A." – that is, Go Big Red, and God Bless America. September 11 opened our eyes to the rest of the world, but some could still only see it from the bleachers.

It wasn't surprising, really, to see this slant. War and its ritual reproduction – football – have always been alike in how they're consumed. The sides are clearly drawn, good and evil are easily distinguishable, enemies are dehumanized. And when it's time to go to battle, the euphoria of the fight floods our mindsets, taking us from a pragmatic realism to a mythic nationalism. But it seems to me that in this conflict, much more than a Big 12 championship is at stake.

Nebraska's win over Rice, though, took place during that extraordinary gray period before things inevitably drifted back to their sharp contrasts – before empty, star-spangled jingoism crept into every crack and crevice of our culture, before we as a nation decided it was easier to wear our game faces forever than to get our minds and hearts around the problem. For one incredible evening, we all stood in Memorial Stadium, hands on heavy hearts as we sang the national anthem, with the sun hanging in the western sky. Though it felt smaller now, the game provided a much-needed reprieve. But darkness eventually fell, and soon enough it was time to go back out into the world.

The Huskersphere

Over the years, numerous suitors have vied for standing as the Big Red's Big Rival. In the '70s it was the Missouri Tigers, who always seemed to practice up on their neck wringing and ankle twisting the week before they played NU. In the '80s and early '90s the Colorado Buffaloes started slinging mud across the state line and circling their calendars in red. And by the end of the century, Kansas State had risen from the primordial ooze to stake its claim too. But try as they might, none of these nouveau riche institutions could ever become Public Enemy No. 1 – they were not the Oklahoma Sooners.

Ask ten Nebraskans who the Huskers' evil twin brother is, and eleven will say Oklahoma. The only disappointing thing about Nebraska's magical run through the 1990s was that Oklahoma wasn't along to put up a fight and add to the mythology of those great years; besieged by probation and constant coaching turmoil, the Sooners were very, very bad while Nebraska subjugated the rest of college football. Watching NU roll up 73-21 and 69-7 victories over the Sooners was sort of like sitting through *Batman and Robin* all the way to the end – you knew the sad events unfolding in front of you were an abomination, but you kept watching anyway out of respect for what had come before.

Eventually Bob Stoops arrived in Norman, installed a spread offense and a growly defense, and restored the Sooner legacy. OU's victory in the 2000 national championship game completed the breathtaking turnaround, and halfway through the following season the Sooners still hadn't been beaten. In October they found themselves sitting atop the BCS standings – one notch higher, in fact, than Dear Old Nebraska U.

It was just like old times; the schools were ripping up opponents, gunning for the national title, and inevitably, locking in on a collision course with everything on the line. NU-OU would be college football's most highly anticipated game of 2001, and rightly so.

This is a really long and convoluted way of saying that when my good friend Don Cox called me from Reno wondering if I could find tickets for the October 27 clash between old rivals, I failed miserably. So he got Texas Tech on October 20 instead.

Cox, though, didn't really mind. Besides being a legendary newspaperman in northern Nevada, he's also the region's biggest sports fan. It doesn't matter – tennis, golf, cricket, rugby, bowling, speed quarters – he loves 'em all. And he's one of those rare cats who loves college football but has no favorite team. He just genuinely loves the pomp and pageantry surrounding the sport.

Years ago, when he was in his thirties, Cox clipped an article in which Beano Cook listed ten things a true college football fan must do before expiring. One is to attend a game at Nebraska. When I was preparing to leave Reno, I invited Cox to visit me in Lincoln and take in a Husker game, figuring I'd probably never see him again. Sure enough, Cox called just a few months later informing me he would be in town.

When I heard of his travel plans, I resolved to show Cox the most festive, most Huskerfied, most red-soaked weekend as humanly possible. And it wasn't difficult: If there's one thing Lincoln has buckets and buckets of, it's atmosphere, tradition, and general pigskin character. Some of it is unique, some of it is hokey, some of it is inspiring, some of it is worthy of a good eye-rolling. But all of it, in at least one small way, gets your Big Red blood pumping.

It starts on Friday, when the red starts to seep onto the downtown sidewalks and streets, and cars with out-of-county license plates begin slowly trolling around, looking for parking spots and driving the wrong way down one-way streets. I know the weekend has officially begun, though, when I see Ed the Scalper (that's what I call him, anyway) hawking tickets on the corner of Ninth and Q streets. It's a Friday custom for me to pass him as I head to Barry's Bar and ask him how much he wants this week. His answer provides a read on whether the average Husker fan feels the next day's opponent is a power or a pushover. Ed was asking seventy-five dollars per ticket, about twenty dollars above face, for Texas Tech. That likely signaled a mid-sized tromping, probably by three touchdowns or so.

I'm not the type of fan who wears my Husker clothes out on Fridays, which puts me in the minority. This is probably because many early arriving fans are out-of-towners, who reflexively throw as many Cornhusker outfits as possible in their suitcases before barreling to Lincoln. Even Cox was wearing a red-and-white "Bugeaters" hat when I met up with him at Barry's, where he had been hanging out for part of the afternoon waiting for me to finish work. He informed me he'd already been to the Nebraska Bookstore, wandered around campus, and eaten a Runza. We separated a couple bottles from their liquids before heading for the Havelock area of town.

Nearly every Lincoln business turns a little red on football weekends. But you'd be hard-pressed to find a place more synonymous with Husker football than Misty's. The Havelock steakhouse featured a sports bar long before every strip mall in the universe was required to house one, and unlike those soulless cookie-cutter joints, Misty's Quarterback Lounge is festooned with actual sports memorabilia that didn't all arrive in the same box. There are helmets, jerseys, and TV sports network banners. There are black-and-white pictures of old university athletes and coaches. There are pennants, signs, and a golden statue of Jerry Tagge behind the bar. On the tables, yellowed clippings extol past Husker glory. It's one of those places in Lincoln where it feels like 1975, 1995, and 2005 all at the same time.

The rest of the restaurant looks like something out of *Goodfellas*. Waitresses in white formal shirts and bow ties tend to patrons sitting in Vegas-style booths, soaking in an ambiance best described as "dark." You can't get this anywhere else in town. And to say Misty's gets a little crowded on Friday evenings is like saying the prime rib is sort of decent: By 8 p.m., it's standing-room-only. You could have a heart attack and you wouldn't hit the ground. Just when you think the fire marshal is going to order the place to shut down, the NU pep band comes busting in, playing "There is No Place Like Nebraska" to roars of approval. Herbie Husker and the Yell Squad are there too, and a raucous pep rally breaks out. Luckily, Cox, Kathy, and I had mowed through our prime rib by the time the pep rally started; it was a lot easier to raise our bottles to the "Go Big Red" chant than it would have been to pump a fork into the air with a chunk of medium-rare meat attached.

We decided to walk off our meals on O Street. We did a bit of bar-hopping ("Huh, so this is where all your football players get in trouble?" Cox asked loudly as we entered the Brass Rail) and eventually landed at Sidetrack Tavern around 10. By this point in the evening on any Friday before a home game, the floor at Sidetrack is good and soaked, and everyone has had enough corn liquor to sing along with the Sidetrack Band's tunes. I credit Cox for being a quick learner; he was belting out lyrics with the rest of the bar within minutes.

In today's TV-beholden world, Football Saturday can take on a variety of forms. As a general rule of thumb, the later the kickoff, the more "juiced" the crowd becomes. If NU plays in the early-bird special on FOX, the pregame action comes from places like Lot 12 or the Vine Street loop, where some of the greatest tailgaters of the modern age reside. If ABC deems Lincoln worthy of a 2:30 p.m. kickoff, however, downtown is exploding with bright red by 10 a.m., campus is alive with sun-visored retirees, and O Street's drinkeries are packed to the rafters. And if it's a night game, as was NU's battle with Texas Tech, the red begins to spread by noon. Despite feeling much the same, each downtown bar takes on a distinct characteristic – Sandy's with its eclectic crowd and urban street corner setting, Barry's with its hard-edged fan base and respectable visitors section, the N Zone with its underground motif and rave-like atmosphere. Eventually, it's time to head to the game.

Campus confers a certain reverence on Football Saturday. Its tall trees line the broad, stone walkways that turn into rivers of red, all converging on Memorial Stadium. Its buildings are, aside from the presence of some dedicated graduate students in Oldfather and Hamilton Halls, dark and lifeless. If you take the main north-south thoroughfare through campus, which starts at the Lied Center and ends on the loop near the entrance to the East Stadium, you walk through a street carnival of sorts. Vendors sell their wares, foot soldiers for social justice shake their charity jars, soapbox preachers warn you of hellfire and eternal damnation. As you approach the grounds, you'll inevitably find scalpers with fistfuls of tickets, and the closer it is to game time the cheaper the tickets are. I once got into an NU-Colorado game for five dollars by hovering until right before kickoff. Most Nebraskans, though, don't like to leave such matters to chance (this genetic anal retentiveness is why you still hear about some lifelong Cornhusker fan in his sixties who in his heart of hearts hopes he'll someday be able to attend a game at Memorial Stadium).

My favorite entry point to campus – to which I became attached during 2001's flawless eight-game home schedule – is a few steps west of the Lied Center, near Kimball Recital Hall and Sheldon Memorial Art Gallery's sculpture garden. There, hundreds of fans watch the Cornhusker Marching Band's mini-performance before it assembles and marches to the stadium. Cox, a big lover of college bands, really grooved on this. The path to the stadium is sort of a Middle Passage between the main on-campus route and a very noisy walk along traffic-filled Tenth Street on the university's western edge. It's a road less taken, to paraphrase the guy named Frost who didn't wear No. 7. The winding, tree-laden path leads you past gorgeous Architecture Hall on your left and Woods Hall on your right, then Brace Lab, Ferguson Hall, and Richards Hall, which was a complete dump when I was in school but is now stately and state-of-the-art, thanks to some serious rehabilitation. Eventually you pop out directly in front of the gates to the south stadium. Cox and I retrieved our tickets and headed in.

This is where, for me, the atmosphere abruptly shifts. Once I'm in earshot of the unmistakable buzz of the pregame crowd, it's all business. As we found our seats, Cox looked around as twilight began to creep in and pronounced Memorial Stadium to his liking. Within minutes, the game was on.

This was one of those contests with every type of crowd noise. When Nebraska roared out to a big first-quarter lead on a bunch of big pass plays, waves of sound emerged from the depths of the stadium floor, as if someone were steadily turning up a stereo system in time for it to crescendo as Tracey Wistrom caught a touchdown pass. When the Blackshirts – who had been unexpectedly put on their heels by the Red Raiders' spread offense – needed a stop on third down, a vibrating, electric wail was directed down from the stands. There were shapeless sounds of seventy-eight thousand people speaking in exasperated unrest as Texas Tech tied the game at half-time. And the truly sublime moments, those plays that turned the game in Nebraska's favor, inspired a sound so loud, so powerful, so sustained that it almost had a feel to it. I'd figured the Huskers would roll, but apparently they wanted to give Cox a bit of a show for all his trouble. NU won 41-31, then slipped off quietly into the night.

We were hungry, so we made our way to – where else? – Valentino's, then headed home. Driving down Normal Boulevard, I turned the radio to the postgame show. The announcers were discussing Keyuo Craver, who was injured against Tech, and whether his injuries would keep him out of the Oklahoma game. I told Cox it was too bad I couldn't get tickets for the big game next week; he smiled and said he'd had a great time nonetheless.

Seven days later, Nebraska upset the Sooners 20-10 behind an inspired defense and Frank Solich's defining moment as head coach: 41 Black Flash Reverse Pass. The double-reverse toss turned Eric Crouch into a receiver in a sudden burst of daring and ingenuity, and after Mike Stuntz hit him for a 63-yard touchdown, Nebraska was on top of the world. But as my friend Peter can attest, I was a complete basket case before, during, and even after the game, pacing and drinking and swearing and yelling odd epithets at my TV for more than four hours. So, as it turns out, it was a really good thing Cox came a week earlier, during NU's dry run for the Sooners. We probably wouldn't have been able to leave the house had he come during Oklahoma Week, and even if we had, I wouldn't have been any damn good to him at all.

The Others

NEBRASKA 11, RICHMOND 6 - JUNE 9, 2002

Of all the sports channels on my Time Warner dial, ESPN Classic is easily the most exciting. Or the least boring, anyway. That's because they can edit out the dead spots of "classic" games, so you rarely have to watch teams trade punts. For years, I wished ESPN Classic could have been in charge of the summer calendar too – that way we could skip May, June, and July and go straight from the Spring Game to Fall Camp. But then one day Nebraska started using aluminum bats to beat up on a bunch of Texans, and summer suddenly didn't seem so god-awful long any more.

I'm referring, of course, to the Big Red baseball team, which in back-to-back campaigns achieved something we never thought was possible: It played in the College World Series. The team had been building for a few years, since Dave Van Horn arrived and began resuscitating the moribund program. In 1999 the Cornhuskers made national headlines by annihilating Chicago State 50-3 in Lincoln, and in 2000 NU came within one game of reaching the CWS.

By the time they broke through in 2001, powering their way to Omaha behind Van Horn's deft management and Shane Komine's telekinetic curveball, the Cornhusker State had officially gone baseball-mad. The mania intensified the following spring, when the team moved from decrepit Buck Beltzer Field to state-of-the-art Haymarket Park. A new dynasty deserved a new field, and in early

147

June nine thousand red-dressed fans crammed into the place to usher Nebraska past the Richmond Spiders in the 2002 NCAA Super Regional.

As the teams warmed up before the decisive Game Three of the series, a joyous electricity coursed through the crowd. It was unlike the murmur of anticipation you hear at Memorial Stadium before a game, though. Instead of impatient grouchiness and an innate feeling of entitlement, Haymarket was filled with a celebratory feeling of accomplishment – the sense that, win or lose, something miraculous already had occurred. The appreciation for how far the team had come in such a short time was evident, so everything the team did well was intoxicating and exhilarating. I wondered as Komine struck out another Richmond batter if this was how Cornhusker football fans felt in the early 1960s, when Bob Devaney rolled into town and made everything new under the sun.

See? Even in June, amid a rowdy baseball crowd, I was thinking about football. In fact, we all were, on one level or another. We can't help it. The football squad is the core team in Nebraska, the origin of all definitions, and we Nebraskans build our view of the university's other athletic squads based on that source. We even wonder how the basketball and volleyball teams can have black in their outfits if the football team doesn't. And that's why when the Huskers finished off Richmond, the most popular T-shirt at Haymarket Park read, "Nebraska – Not Just Football!" The shirt was well intentioned, to be sure, but if I were a member of the Husker baseball team, I'd probably be a bit offended.

I'd be bothered too if I were a die-hard Husker baseball fan who suddenly had to put up with unremitting frontrunners wearing Fiesta Bowl caps and Eric Crouch jerseys next to me. Before Van Horn made baseball hip, you could always count on a couple hundred dyed-in-the-wool fans to brave the early-March chill and yell for the team. On each Friday in the autumn, a thousand people also flock to Abbott Sports Complex in northeast Lincoln to chant "Goal Big Red." The NU volleyball team regularly sells out the Coliseum. The wrestlers, women's hoopsters, and gymnasts all inspire a committed following. And none of those fans enjoy having their favorite group of Cornhuskers defined as some cute little subset of the football team.

What strikes me most about the "other" sports is the familiarity with one another they all seem to share. Sitting at a Husker soccer match, you hear discussions about the wrestling team. At a wrestling meet, you hear talk of the women's basketball team. At a women's basketball game, the people two rows down are discussing Husker softball. At a softball game, there are conversations about NU soccer. And no matter what sport you're watching, everyone calls the athletes by their first names.

That's when you realize two types of people wear the red: the football fans and the school loyalists. The groups aren't mutually exclusive, of course – nearly all school loyalists are football fans, for example, though football fans, as the name implies, love Husker football and little else. To them UNL is nothing more than a necessary vessel to house the football program and to provide a satellite transmission of their white-helmeted heroes to their basement war rooms every Saturday. School loyalists, meanwhile, draw their fandom from their involvement, experience, and pride in the state's flagship university.

I'm in the school loyalist camp. I will root, root, root for the home team, no matter what, because I am genuinely attached to my equality-engendering, diversity-promoting, progressive-thinking state university. The teams NU puts on the playing fields are totems of these feelings, and when they compete they always manage to arouse in me those deeply held scarlet-and-cream values, the ones that make me believe that no matter what, the Cornhuskers are always on the right side. This is something I've learned about myself since moving home, as I've found my place among the folksy volleyball crowd. And the suburban, minivan-driving soccer crowd. And the youthful, rap-metal basketball crowd. And, of course, the joyful, euphoric baseball crowd – like the one that celebrated giddily after NU secured another trip to Omaha by beating Richmond.

I know it requires a measure of blind allegiance to always, always, always cheer for Nebraska, whether it's in baseball or bowling or tiddly-winks. I know the support I give these "other" sports is more of a reflexive loyalty, too, at least compared to the full-blown worship I practice for the football team. I know I probably care more about the color of a uniform than the actual significance of the sporting event I'm watching. Would I tune to FOX Sports Net and watch the NCAA volleyball Final Four in its entirety if Nebraska wasn't playing? Good gravy, man, not a chance. But here's something else I know: I'll always see the red-and-white outfits as an absolute good. I'll always keep an emotional investment in those who wear them. I'll always relish their victories, and I'll always share in their defeats.

Good Grief

As the 2002 season approached, a colleague noted the Cornhuskers' season would probably hinge on the results of five games. "Five goddamn games," he huffed. "When was the last time you heard someone say that?"

Well, never. The suggestion that five opponents on Nebraska's schedule had a valid shot at beating the Huskers was almost beyond comprehension. In Lincoln, football seasons were traditionally defined by one make-or-break weekend in late November, with the other ten games serving as mere pretense. Everything built up to the day after Thanksgiving, which would either see an historic championship victory or (all too often) a cataclysmic defeat. One big game – that's about all the buildup and stress we Husker fans were conditioned to expect in a single year.

Of course, in August the usual bloc of Eager Believers bought plane tickets for the Big 12 championship game. Those who paid close attention in the off season, however, were sensing something else – something subtle and unformed but ominous nonetheless. You picked it up by watching how players carried themselves, by listening to how coaches chose their words with the media. A malaise had fallen over Memorial Stadium. The program was not moving forward.

It probably would have helped our peace of mind if the Cornhuskers hadn't been beaten in their final two games of the 2001 season. Let me rephrase that. It probably would have helped our peace of mind if the Cornhuskers hadn't been completely blasted in their final two games of the 2001 season. First, on what became known as Black Friday, Colorado crushed the Big Red in Boulder. The Buffs rang up the most points ever on a Nebraska team, snatched the Big 12 North title, and obliterated NU's perfect season in one fell swoop. Still, the Bowl Championship Series thought it amusing to pit NU against No. 1 Miami for the national championship. It took the Hurricanes just over a quarter to grab hold of what remained of the

Cornhuskers from the Boulder debacle, crumple them like aluminum cans, and toss them aside on their way to the Sears Trophy. The
two losses inflicted so much psychic damage, in fact, that it over-
shadowed the final games in red for Eric Crouch, whom the Big Red
had leaned on so often for four solid years.

By the following fall, underused understudy Jammal Lord had
taken over the reins. You had to squint pretty hard to recognize the
Nebraska offense early in the 2002 season. Mainly, it consisted of
Lord dropping to throw, feeling pressure almost instantly, fleeing the
pocket, dodging a linebacker, and getting dragged down after a short
gain. Even when the line gave Lord time to pass, he wasn't exactly
evoking images of Dave Humm or Vince Ferragamo. McCathorn
Clayton, maybe. On the other side of the ball, Craig Bohl's Blackshirts were laboring to get out from under the "too slow" tag since
Miami sped past them nine months earlier. Still, the team was winning, and conventional wisdom said three warm-up games at Memorial Stadium – Arizona State, Troy State, Utah State – would give
them enough time to gel before taking on Penn State in Happy Valley.

Well, it was a nice theory, anyway.

Once the shock of getting thrashed by 33 points by the Nittany
Lions wore off, the realization swept across the state that the next
opponent, Iowa State, had suddenly become the game of the year.
Win, and NU could possibly salvage its season. Lose, and . . . well, it
was best not to go there.

But Nebraska was never in the game in Ames. The only bright spot
was midway through the first half, with the Cornhuskers trailing and
at their own 10. Lord began to run an option play, then retreated and
lofted a pass to Ross Pilkington. The freshman split end got behind
the Cyclone defense and raced for a 90-yard touchdown – and that
was it, the lone highlight of the afternoon. The listless Huskers lost
consecutive regular-season games for the first time since I was five.

It wasn't even October yet, but the season was kaput. Everyone, on
some level at least, knew this to be true as NU staggered off the field.
Eight games remained, and from what we had seen, the Big Red
would be lucky to win half. *Luck* – that's even lower in the fan cache
than *hope*. We had done plenty of hoping over the years: that NU
could beat Oklahoma at the end of the season, that the Huskers
could get another shot at the national title, that enough voters in the

coaches' poll would award the Big Red a share. But hope died that day at Jack Trice Stadium. It was all over – maybe for good.

In fact, I recall a vast majority of the weather in the fall of 2002 as being cold and gray and dreary, with daylight-saving time seemingly ending months earlier than normal. I wonder now if this is a just a trick of memory, but really – how could the sun have shone at all that autumn when I felt so *awful* all the time? Living and working in the epicenter of it all, surrounded by daily reminders of how desperate things had become, was a heavy burden. For a good chunk of September and October, Lincoln felt empty, bland, and more hushed than ever, even on Football Saturdays. I felt perpetually exhausted but strangely anxious at the same time. Work dragged on forever, and coworkers with whom I had never had problems before suddenly grated on my nerves. I drank and ate too much, got angry at the slightest inconvenience, and took out my frustrations in all the wrong places. And you know what? Compared to some people, I took the Huskers' crash pretty *well*.

I mean, to my friends and family, I'm the most rabid, most obsessive Nebraska backer on the planet, and to them my obligation to the Cornhuskers (season tickets, never missing a televised road game, a bowl trip every two or three years) is without peer. But I don't travel to away games, I'm not inclined to buy something just because it has a red *N* on it, I'd never rummage through musty old practice gear at the athletic department's annual garage sale, I don't go to Photo Day so I can get a picture of the new walk-ons, and I can think of a hundred things better to do on a weeknight than to watch game film at Holy Ghost Church in Omaha. I recognize my location in the Holy Spectrum of Husker Fans, and I know my level of mania doesn't even register on some scales. I was a big fan but not nearly the biggest. I'd seen enough of the world to put the whole Husker thing into perspective, and upon returning to Nebraska I realized there are many people who use Nebraska football fandom as one of their defining characteristics, like "Catholic" or "Czech." Despite my angst, I could still view the mess with a measure of academic detachment. They could not. I could only imagine what grisly scenes were playing out in some quarters of the state.

It is widely accepted by psychologists, psychiatrists, and other really smart people that upon suffering a tremendous loss, human beings go through five very distinct stages of grief: denial, bargaining, anger, despair, and, at last, acceptance. Sociologists wondering if that model worked on a mass scale needed to look no further than the Cornhusker State in 2002.

Denial. In the season's early weeks, all uneasiness was quelled by our magical logic: *We always win because we are Mighty Nebraska, and we are Mighty Nebraska because we always win.* Even when Penn State laid that five-touchdown slobberknocking on NU, there was an effort to rationalize it away by cobbling together a winding list of key plays – dropped Husker passes, blown calls by the officials, turnovers that shouldn't have been turnovers – that would have negated the loss had they *all* gone the Huskers' way. Oddly, these same folks scoffed at PSU's "1994 National Champions" banner on their way out of Beaver Stadium.

Bargaining. After Iowa State plowed through the Big Red, the preferred activity was to shop around for a cure-all for the team's woes. First fans called for Mike Stuntz, who performed gamely against the Cyclones after Lord was yanked in the second half. Then it was Curt Dukes, the heralded freshman from North Carolina. This led to suggestions that Turner Gill, now the quarterbacks coach under Frank Solich but without an iota of offensive coordinator experience, should take over play calling duties. And by mid-season, relentless calls for Red Outs at Memorial Stadium were radiating from the South Stadium offices, urging fans to eschew white, black, or gray Husker gear in favor of head-to-toe red. This somehow suggested that if we fans went above and beyond on Football Saturday, then the Cornhuskers would do the same.

But nothing worked.

Anger. The boiling point came in October, when Nebraska lost to Oklahoma State for the first time in four decades. A wave of blistering fury roared across the state, with scapegoats so ample there almost wasn't time to get to them all: the offensive line, with its uninspired off-the-ball surge and its sagging waistlines; Bohl, who had turned the Blackshirts into the Blackskirts; Lord, whose passes were so inaccurate it would make a FOX News anchor green with envy; Lord, who indefensibly *cracked a smile* on camera as the final, bitter seconds ticked away in Stillwater; Lord, who childishly spurned the media, apparently in protest of what he felt was unfair coverage; Lord, who by the end of the season had been linked to a flagging state economy, low crop prices, and global warming too.

But most of all, the anger fell upon Solich. He was, after all, the Man, the Guy in Charge, the Keeper of the Flame, the inevitable end point of every frustrated barroom debate. He had been determined to be the sum of all the Huskers' broken parts, a label he did nothing to dispel as he stood each week on the sideline, looking powerless and clueless and feckless as streak after vaunted NU streak met its demise.

Despair. At the end of the regular season, Nebraska got plunked by Colorado again, dropping its record to 7-6. The day after the loss, the *Lincoln Journal Star*'s front-page headline read "Now Is the Winter of Our Discontent." Word was that several assistant coaches were getting the ax, and even thinking about how to salvage anything from the chaos that was my once-proud football program was flat-out exhausting. Predictions of losing seasons well into the foreseeable future coursed through area newsprint and computer screens. One Internet poster even compared the emotional damage inflicted by the 2002 season to his reaction to the September 11 attacks. For a while there, the only thing missing was an old man wearing a sandwich board and yelling out verses from the book of Revelations.

Acceptance. In the weeks and months that followed, a sort of perspective emerged. Old-timers talked about enduring the Bill Jennings era in apparent attempts to put things in a historical point of view, but their stories rarely contained any clear messages, except to say that losing football games in the 1960s felt pretty much the same as losing football games in the twenty-first century. Others sought refuge in waxing nostalgic about the glory days, sighing and evoking images of Jerry Tagge stretching across the goal line, Johnny the Jet's punt return, Tommie Frazier's spectacular run. And I have to admit, that helped for a while. But nostalgia is really a useless human emotion; it's just a temporary tranquilizer for defeated souls. And no matter what kind of perspective you put on what had happened to the Cornhuskers, that's where you always ended up: defeat.

I suppose the obvious lesson we learned in 2002 – and in many ways, again in 2004 – was to appreciate all of the team's wins, not just the ones against Oklahoma and Colorado for the league title. But it was a hard thing, admitting we were lowering our standards like that. Deep down I think we all believe our high expectations up in the stands help yield championship results down on the field. Redefining our meaning of success was copping out, letting the team down.

But shouldn't it have been really easy? Wasn't football, as Tom Osborne famously opined, supposed to be about more than wins and losses? One day in April, my friend Corey gave me the answer to that question: "More than winning sure sounds nice, man. When you're winning."

He made me think about when I was a kid, when I used to wonder what it would be like in the land of America's Greatest Fans if the Cornhuskers ever fell from their lofty perch. But I could never really, truly picture it – after all, it was something that could only happen in theory, like cold fusion or a liberal Unicameral. But if the day ever came, the assumption was that we Nebraska fans, we great stoics of the Great Plains, would deal with it in the quiet, resolute manner that our team inspired. That mythology, however, was punctured early and often. We suffered through the same bitter denial, resentment, and depression the earthbound mortals at Oklahoma, USC, and Notre Dame felt when their respective dynasties fell.

The reaction from our unique red society was probably more pronounced, in fact, given those of us younger than forty considered winning a birthright and not a privilege. Precisely because we'd never gone through something so awful before, the intensity of our panic, our anxiety, and our outrage was something you didn't see at any old school whose football team went .500. So in that way the 2002 season proved that we Nebraska fans are, indeed, unique. But boy, when you get right down to it, it also showed that we're nothing special.

We Don't Know the Words

TEXAS 27, NEBRASKA 24 - NOVEMBER 2, 2002

Many times, usually after Nebraska has dropped a woulda-coulda-shoulda heartbreaker, I've wished I had the power to travel back in time. First, I'd go back and fix NU's most recent tragedy, but I wouldn't stop there: I'd then retreat through the decades and impose some extreme red-clad justice on the bastards who beat the Huskers unfairly over the years. Given a time machine and, say, a piece of metal pipe, there's no date in Husker history – the loss to Florida State on January 1, 1994, for example – that I couldn't rectify.

It's a good thing for Charlie Ward's kneecaps, though, that the only proven way to travel through time is forward, one plodding second at a time. The closest we can come to time travel is with our memories, I suppose, and even then we can't always control when and where we're going to go. Every time I smell chicken being barbecued, for example, I'm swept back to my boyhood, running around with my friend Monty near the chicken pit at the annual Thurston County Old Settlers Picnic. I seem to go there a lot these days because of my next-door neighbor's brand-new outdoor grill.

To me music is an even more powerful tool in this regard. "Up, Up, and Away" by the Fifth Dimension sends me all the way back to age six, to Jim's Market in Bancroft with my mom, buying groceries. Wang Chung's "Everybody Have Fun Tonight," which in retrospect is a really crappy song, still transports me to age sixteen, and I'm riding in my sister's Ford Escort down Dodge Street with her and her Omaha friends. OMC's "How Bizarre" blasts me ahead another decade, as Kathy and I barrel north on Interstate 5 toward San Francisco, and I've just told a joke that she's laughing at. These images are sharp and clear to me, and I find a certain comfort in them.

That makes sense, I suppose. Music stimulates all kinds of parts in the brain, giving both the right and left hemispheres plenty to do when a song drifts our way. One side codifies lyrics, for example, while the other tries to break down melody. Because we can't actually see or touch music, our brains have to use all kinds of feelings and imagery to interpret it. That's why, experts say, music has the potent ability to generate emotions, memories, and images, and set them as a sort of soundtrack to the random slideshows of our lives.

When I hear "There Is No Place Like Nebraska," however, I can't say I get transported to any particular time or place. Sure, I can think of a few big games in which the song is present in my memory, but none of them serve as the central recollection for the song. It would be difficult to attach a specific memory to such an eternal anthem as "There is No Place Like Nebraska," after all. I learned it along with my nursery rhymes. The song has always been there.

It's an absurdly simple song – just a customary march in 4/4 time. But all the same, I can't hope to wrap my brain around it. Our school song evokes too many feelings, too many sentiments, too many deep-seated passions to try to define it. So I'm content not to question it and just let it do what it was meant to do – make my heart feel a little bolder with each passing note. It's never failed me, no matter what the venue, the situation, or the manner in which it is being played. I have similar feelings for "Hail Varsity," "March of the Cornhusker," "Glory of the Gridiron," and "March Grandioso" as well – inside the stadium, those tunes are essential survival tools, even if Husker-Vision drowns them out half the time. My experiences of everything else on Football Saturday would be less vivid without them.

But there's more music surrounding Nebraska football than the brassy, iconic harmonies of the Pride of All Nebraska, and plenty of it appeals to our need for relatively senseless enjoyment. As evidence of this phenomenon, please allow me to submit the banshees at Sidetrack Tavern, a dark, windowless dive on O Street between Ninth and Tenth streets.

On the Fridays before a Husker home game, Sidetrack becomes a crush of humanity that sweats, drinks, and sings in unison. Leading the sing-along is the famous Sidetrack Band, led by Joyce Durand on keyboard and Paul "Fig" Newton on guitar. Durand opened the bar in 1977 down by the railroad tracks at Seventh and P (hence the name), but it's been at its current location since 1985. Each week the band runs through a lengthy list of football tunes and parodies of other popular songs. Fig's rhyming lyrics are salty enough to make a sailor blush. Let's put it this way, the Sidetrack Band really hated to see Mike Rucker graduate.

The joint always reminds me of a scene in *Road House*, in which the inimitable Patrick Swayze plays a bouncer at a rural Missouri drink-n-puke. When he refuses entry to three troublemakers by telling them his obviously hopping nightclub is closed, one of the bad guys grunts, "Closed? Then what the hell are all these people doing in here?" Swayze answers, "They're drinking and having a good time." And that pretty much sums up the deep philosophy of life at Sidetrack. It is truly a visceral experience, a live-in-the-moment sort of environment you just have to see for yourself, and one you can't duplicate at a tacky, one-size-fits-all sports bar in a strip mall out in the new part of town. At Sidetrack, the hair is bad, the beer is bad, the floors are sticky by nine o'clock, and no one gives a damn. Fig and Joyce's salacious tunes turn the bar into a giant karaoke shrine to Nebraska football, and that's music to everyone's ears.

It says a lot about Sidetrack's melodic magic that Kathy, who would rather have her eyes poked out with burning sticks than have anything to do with the Nebraska Cornhuskers, loves the place and insisted on going there the night before Nebraska took on Texas in

Lincoln. My theory is Kathy enjoys it because Sidetrack is tied to the Huskers only in a cultural sense. There's no serious football talk going on, no obsessive breaking down of tomorrow's two-deep rosters, no in-depth debates over the intricacies of the Bowl Championship Series formula. That's too high-minded, man, especially when we can all stand up instead and belt out the bar's official version of "Hail Varsity," which goes like this:

> We don't know the words.
> No, we don't know the words.
> We don't know the words.
> We don't know the words.

The next evening, Kathy attended a much more highbrow musical function, a vocal recital at Seward High School in which my teenaged nephew and niece took part. I didn't go. In fact, two weeks earlier when she found out that the kickoff for the Texas game was within a half-hour of the recital, she simply shrugged and told me she'd see me Sunday morning. It's been long accepted by my family and friends that my social calendar is built around Nebraska football, and they know I'm not going to be at any dinner parties, weddings, or other social engagements scheduled against a home game. Or, let's be realistic here, *any* game. I'm sure they hate it, because I'm being selfish. I hate it, too, because they're right – I am being selfish. But I'm still going to watch the game.

As my friend Corey and I slid into our north stadium seats, the band was in the middle of its pregame show. We'd spent a little extra time at Sandy's, see, and we were a little extra primed for the big game. When the band began playing "March Grandioso," we noticed two Texas fans in front of us cheering and doing the insipid "Hook 'em Horns" sign. Corey wondered out loud what in the hell those two thought they were doing to our song. Someone behind us said that Texas uses "March Grandioso" in its pregame show as well.

"Sunsabitches," I said. "They ruin everything."

Well, *en vino, veritas.* I can't say I like Texas very much. In their first four meetings as Big 12 rivals, Texas beat Nebraska three times. Longhorn fans were snotty enough just on the basis of being Longhorn fans, but now they had scoreboard domination as well. And in 2002 Texas fielded a vastly superior team to the Huskers, and the only thing the Big Red had going for it was home-field advantage. Now here were the Texans in the crowd, festooned in outfits of baby-poop orange, stealing a chunk of it right out from under us, like they owned the song or something. If they knew they shared a musical march with the Cornhuskers, they'd probably drop it like an old hanky. Like I said, sunsabitches.

Nebraska got blown out of its share of ballgames in 2002. But its loss to Texas was not one of those games. The Cornhuskers, who had won twenty-six consecutive games at Memorial Stadium, were not going to go down without a good fight. And Jammal Lord, the much-maligned quarterback, had the game of his young career, running through, over, and around the Longhorns on his way to a school record for rushing yards by a quarterback. Still, the Horns' Chris Simms was having a career day, throwing for something like 2,981 yards – OK, it was only 419 – against the Blackshirts. Texas appeared to have capped a "ballgame" drive with three minutes left when Cedric Benson went over from two yards out to put UT up 27-17. But the Huskers answered a minute later to pull within three. Miraculously, they then forced Texas to punt. There was less than a minute to go.

Then Texas coach Mack Brown showed exactly why he has so much trouble winning the big one: He allowed the ball to be kicked to DeJuan Groce. In a season full of disappointment, No. 5 had shined – DeJuan already had run three punts back for scores in '02, and as he gathered the ball and made a quick juke, Corey smacked me on the arm and screamed, "There he goes!"

Groce weaved and sped down the field, dodging white-clad Longhorns like he was running into traffic on the interstate. When someone finally caught him, he was at the Texas 16. The stands were shaking and vibrating with pure sound. On the Huskers' first play, Lord kept for no gain. Twenty, nineteen, eighteen . . . on second down, he spiked the ball to stop the clock. Sixteen ticks were left. On third down, No. 10 fired the ball toward the corner of the end zone, toward freshman Mark LeFlore, who had momentarily flashed into the open – but the pass was intercepted by cornerback Nathan Vasher. Ballgame, Texas.

For a moment, Corey and I considered putting a thumping on some nearby Texas fans who were waving their Lone Star flag and embracing in a series of lengthy man-hugs, but instead we shuffled toward the exit in mock indignation. The Longhorns, a Top 10 team, had just pulled a victory out of their asses over an unranked, 6-4 ball club, and these two were celebrating as if their team had just won the Super Bowl. It was time to leave.

Corey and I wandered to Sandy's, but once the adrenaline wore off and the reality of the loss started to settle in, our beers didn't seem quite as cold. So we wandered down O Street until we found ourselves at the entrance of Sidetrack Tavern. You could hear the music pumping from the street. We went inside.

Joyce, Fig, and the band were in full swing, cranking out tunes and doing their best to get through all the requests on the bar napkins. Everyone around us was nursing cans of Bud or Miller Lite. Joyce was at the mike, telling her best Oklahoma Sooner jokes. Corey and I stood in the back of the bar for a while and did our best to sing along with our raw throats.

We had fun for a while, but it was a muted sort of amusement. Every time a Longhorn fan entered, we were reminded of what had just happened. I told Corey I wished I had that time machine so I could go back and repair that final Husker drive. Or better yet, go back to the night before, so we could actually enjoy the Sidetrack Band. Corey nodded, downed the rest of his beer, and said it was getting late. It wasn't, not really. Still, I concurred, and I followed him back outside, into the silence.

Hook, Line, and Husker Nation

NEBRASKA 17, OKLAHOMA STATE 7 – AUGUST 30, 2003

We Nebraskans tend to think of ourselves as sort of wry, like the clever small-town folks in movies such as *Doc Hollywood* or *Funny Farm*. In those flicks, the townspeople pretend to be all simple and unassuming, as the rural typecast goes, but turn out to be quite shrewd and manipulative in the end. We love movies where naive, urban nancy-boys who can't drive tractors get what's coming to them because it reinforces some of our core self-beliefs: We are smart; we are discerning; we are intuitive. And by virtue of being born in the central part of the North American land mass, we all have the magical ability to detect bullshit in all its forms.

Few things rankle us more, then, than an outsider coming in and trying to show us backward-thinking rubes how things are done out in the Real World. Anyone who takes this tack, and who speaks freely of it, will meet swift and biting resistance, as Bill Byrne most assuredly understands. As NU's athletic director, Byrne presided over the most prolific era in Nebraska football history, but even three Sears trophies couldn't truly get him into the good graces of the red masses. He wasn't one of us, see. He was from Oregon, where they don't farm a whole lot, they vote for Democrats, and they throw the football. His pedigree didn't mesh with our family tree.

Byrne's already short slack tightened even more in 2002, when he was asked if the Huskers' poor season was hurting cash donations to the athletic department. Byrne's reply, which actually contained the words "boosters of substance," suggested he was only concerned with what the fat-cat donors thought. It also suggested Byrne wasn't going to be around much longer, one way or another: In December he bolted to Texas A&M. For the record, there was no farewell parade along O Street, and as per our instructions, Byrne did not let the door hit him on his way out of town.

The disdain we have for outsiders, however, is directly proportional to the admiration we bestow upon our Prodigal Sons. We have infinite respect and regard for native Nebraskans who leave the state as young adults, make names for themselves in other places, and eventually return to apply their worldly expertise. Our statewide feelings of inadequacy place a powerful mystique on the outside world and those who are brave enough to go out into it. Those who do this enjoy a nearly mythical down-home gravitas upon their return. They become, for want of a better term, cosmopolitan good ol' boys. And that's a damn tough quality to beat, especially if you're up against one of these guys for the job of athletic director at the University of Nebraska.

The son of a state senator, Steve Pederson came from North Platte by way of Pittsburgh. He started out as an NU sports–information assistant and spent four years in the '80s as recruiting coordinator before leaving for similar jobs at Ohio State and Tennessee. He returned in 1994 as Byrne's associate athletic director for football but left again two years later to become Pittsburgh's AD. And over the next seven years, as the Pittsburgh media is fond of telling us, he turned the Panthers' waning athletic program into a winner.

Byrne, in giving Nebraskans an emphatic "up yours" during his final autumn in Lincoln, had left the door wide open for Pederson.

Pederson didn't walk through, he sprinted. If Byrne was the elitist, then Pederson would be the populist: He repeatedly called on the "1.7 million walk-ons" to resurrect the football program. He directed his focus (publicly, at least) on fan-related matters Byrne would have seen as peripheral and unimportant. He deep-sixed the disastrous, Spandex-gusset uniforms the Cornhuskers wore to their dooms in 2002. He transformed Herbie Husker from a moth-eaten fleabag to a muscle-bound Disney character. He replaced the rotting wooden bleachers with nice Fiberglas ones. He symbolically trimmed ticket prices a few bucks. And as the season approached, he ordered signs placed above each Memorial Stadium entrance that said, "Through These Gates Pass the Greatest Fans in College Football."

And we seasoned skeptics, we independent-thinking Nebraskans? We ate this stuff up. We're suckers for a little attention, after all. What's funny is that in the grand scheme of things, not much had changed: The jury was still out on Solich as head coach; Jammal Lord was still taking snaps; the offensive line was still about as tough as tinfoil. But for the first time in a long time, things felt like they were moving again, and therefore, they felt important. Steve Pederson had provided that momentum, though it barely took a glance to realize his aesthetic changes weren't exactly fundamental reforms.

It didn't matter. We were ready to believe again. Lord, were we ready. After a nightmarish '02 season, a hero was needed in the worst way. Pederson, we reasoned, bore all the markings. As summer began to creep to a close, we convinced ourselves we'd found the champion we'd been searching for since Tom Osborne walked away six years earlier. Finally – we had someone like us in control of our collective fates. Pederson did all he could to seize upon and solidify this perception. His early tenure at Nebraska assumed the look and feel of a political campaign, with high-profile press conferences bearing no real news becoming commonplace and stump speeches being read to cheers at red-clad rallies around the state.

Pederson's first year back at NU also was a clear lesson in the power of language and how it can be used to stoke certain feelings and provoke certain reactions. In this case, it was the term "Husker Nation," an umbrella phrase Pederson used to describe anyone who even remotely followed the Cornhuskers. This colloquialism had been floating around for nearly a decade before Pederson officialized it in early 2003. The earliest usage I can remember was 1995, when

Howard Schnellenberger took over at Oklahoma and created the "Sooner Nation" rallying cry. Schnellenberger lasted only a year at OU, but "Sooner Nation" and all its bastard forms lived on, spreading beyond Norman to other schools.

It was a perfect sports cliché that supporters of any run-of-the-mill team could evoke in three short steps: 1) Say your school's mascot; 2) add "Nation"; 3) Voila! Your fan base has a newly manufactured sense of definition and unity. I knew for sure the expression had played out nationally when I ran into some Coastal Carolina fans in town for an NCAA baseball regional, and they actually referred to themselves as "Chanticleer Nation." I'm not kidding.

It appeared "Husker Nation" had run its course in the local vernacular as well. That was, until Pederson began repeating the term like a Gregorian chant in every interview, press conference, press release, and speaking engagement in 2003. Like other highly branded buzzwords that get parroted by the media – Shock and Awe, New Democrat, War on Terror, It's the Economy Stupid – it took little time for "Husker Nation" to spread quickly back into the language. Before you knew it, the cliché was en vogue again, symbolizing our solidarity as we prepared for the rebirth of our football program.

And what's wrong with that? Well, nothing, I suppose. Just like there's nothing wrong with eating at T.G.I.Fridays or Applebees. It does show, however, how susceptible we really are to slick packaging, relentless marketing, and pre-manufactured enthusiasm, despite our claims to the contrary. In short, we like bells. Whistles too. That goes double if said bells and whistles have red *N*s on them and carry the message that we Nebraskans are a good, moral people, that we're special in our football fandom. And that by being this way, we somehow have a direct influence on the outcome of Nebraska's football games.

Undoubtedly, this shoulder-shrugging acceptance of such marketing campaigns is a generational thing. I'm unashamedly a member of Generation X, and our cynicism – along with our *Mellon Collie and the Infinite Sadness* CDs – is our most prized possession. Until Generation Y came around, we were the most marketed-to group in American history and so we've built up quite the immunity to schmaltz. It insults our intelligence to be pandered to by posers. To us there's a fine line between authenticity and posturing. Many people older and younger than us – Nebraskan or otherwise – do not perceive, or care to perceive, this phenomenon. Those folks? They gladly bought "Husker Nation" T-shirts, believing with every particle of their beings that it was a proud emblem of their vastly superior value system. But when I saw them strolling past, I couldn't help but think: *Suckers.*

Amid all this hoopla Frank Solich was preparing his Huskers for the first game of 2003. As it neared, a renewed sense of urgency had wound through the Cornhusker camp. Solich had brought on six new assistants to stop the bleeding from 2002, including hotshot defensive coordinator Bo Pelini, a transplant from the Green Bay Packers. Like everyone else in the state, I was dying to see how this was going to play out. The opponent, Oklahoma State, had a powerful offense and was ranked in the season's first poll. Nebraska, for the first time since the Ice Age, was not. ABC Sports found this intriguing enough to come to town. It was not your typical August opener.

I sat in the North Stadium with my coworker Don, who graciously loaned me his second ticket. We arrived a good hour before kickoff; Don suggested we get to the stadium early because of an expected crush of up to ten thousand extra fans around the grounds. This was because of another Pederson innovation called the Husker Nation Pavilion. Modeled after a similar brainchild at Pittsburgh, the Pavilion is an area northeast of the stadium where people who apparently don't have tickets can stand around in red and watch a feed of the game on a big screen. There's also live music, Pepsi products, and best I can tell, lots of children named Morgan, Jordan, and Taylor getting their faces painted.

I hope none of these kids were near my section that day. If they were, they undoubtedly learned a few new words. Nebraska gave up a couple of big plays early to the Pokes and fell behind. But the Blackshirts eventually settled down, and by the third quarter NU trailed just 7-3. The problem was the offense was still wandering around without a clue, prompting Don to say, "I think the defense is going to have to score."

Not five minutes later, with everyone on their feet, OSU had possession on its own 15. Cowboy quarterback Josh Fields handed the ball to Tatum Bell, and somehow the ball came free. A white-clad Cowboy saw it there and began to turn toward it, but suddenly it was in someone's hands – someone in red! No. 38, linebacker Barrett Ruud, was rumbling away, past two stunned Cowboys, down the east sideline, and into the end zone. The stadium erupted. Nebraska had pushed into the lead.

There are different kinds of touchdowns – long ones, which you know are going to be touchdowns several seconds before the ball carrier crosses the goal line. And athletic ones, which make you wonder how a human being can pull off such incredible physical feats. There are satisfyingly clever ones, which come on innovative plays that fool the opponent. And then there are the cathartic ones like Ruud's, those liberating tallies during tight contests where every play literally counts, that happen in a blink of an eye and blast the crowd into the stratosphere. These are the sweetest touchdowns of all.

NU grabbed another fumble later in the quarter, and Jammal Lord and Co. finished off a short drive to put the Cornhuskers up 10. Slowly but surely over the next fifteen minutes, the Huskers killed off the game, mixing a ball-control offense with their suffocating defense to earn the season's first win. In the D, the glory: The Cowboys' all-America wideout, Rashaun Woods, was held to just five catches. OSU's running game disappeared in the second half. And Fields, who had ripped the Blackshirts a year earlier, was perplexed by Pelini's blitzes and zone coverages.

It was a vintage Nebraska win, like those great Big 8 slugfests of old, when something deep inside the team would rise up, generate a game-turning play, elevate the Big Red to victory, and affirm our devotion to the team. It felt good to win one like this, in such a traditional, poetic fashion. For the first time in a couple of years, I wasn't sure if I could wait seven whole days to see the Big Red in action again.

Don and I left the stadium, and I decided to head toward the Nebraska Union. Other pleased and relieved fans were pouring out of the turnstiles, marveling over NU's gutsy effort. As I passed the bronze statue near the Vine Street loop, a middle-aged guy in red climbed atop, raised his left fist to the sky, and screamed, "HUSKER NATION!"

The crowd around him let out a cheer. Before I realized what I was doing, I raised my left fist back toward him, in some sort of offhand, improvised patriotic salute, and yelled along with the others.

Somewhere, high above Memorial Stadium in his skybox, Steve Pederson was smiling.

At Game's End

It was that point in the game again. Colorado quarterback Joel Klatt had just picked out Derek McCoy for a 17-yard score, and what had been an 11-point Cornhusker lead had swung to a 1-point Buffalo advantage. Folsom Field was pulsating as the grass-stained Blackshirts trudged off the field, heads bowed and hands on hips. More than ten minutes remained in the third quarter, but everyone in red knew the game was done.

This had happened so many times lately, after all. The Cornhuskers would be in the contest, battling gamely, when a play here and a play there would go against them. But instead of using the situation as an opportunity to step it up, they would collapse. This scenario, which had quickly become a hallmark of the Frank Solich era, had occurred three times already in losses to Missouri, Texas, and just two weeks earlier, Kansas State. And now, in Boulder, it was happening again.

Only it didn't. At some watershed moment after that score, a tiny white-hot flame lit inside the Cornhuskers. They started carrying themselves with more urgency and purpose. The Blackshirts seized the game's momentum by crashing in on Klatt and stifling the Buffs' pass-happy attack. Meanwhile, NU's offense began to steadily move the football. And in the fourth quarter, the Huskers intercepted CU twice, rallied for 10 unanswered points, and notched their ninth win of the year.

On the sidelines, Solich got Gatoraded; back home the offices of the *Lincoln Journal Star* got egged – just days earlier, the newspaper had reported the athletic director had secretly told high-placed boosters he wanted Solich gone. Apparently, rational and irrational Husker fans alike saw the 31-22 victory as proof the report was wrong and the head coach would live to fight another day.

The newspaper, though, hit the story right on the screws. The next day, Steve Pederson lowered the boom on Frank Solich, firing him after six chaotic seasons as head coach of the Cornhuskers. Fifty-eight wins, nineteen losses, a Big 12 title, and an appearance in the '01 national title game weren't enough. Not at Nebraska.

The football fan in me, the magical thinker who believes it is the Huskers' destiny to triumph in every game, was not exactly stunned that this had gone down. The Nebraskan in me, however, was – and it was that part that boiled to the surface that Saturday evening when news of the firing rolled off my answering machine. I was shocked and stunned; I felt betrayed and unappreciated. In other words, I felt as if I had been fired along with Frank Solich.

Why? The connection a Husker fan shares with the head coach can be incredibly strong, even stronger than the one we share with players. Players come and go, passing through our consciousness for four or five years and then fading away. There are some who are good and some who are great, and there are some who are immortal, whose legends grow with each passing year. But they're just players; they can't affect us in the constant manner coaches can. Coaches, like longtime bosses and two-term presidents, leave a thumbprint. They're always there, working toward some far-off goal, and as a fan you can always claim to know better than them, but deep down you know that in the long run, his choices and evaluations are infinitely better than yours.

This relationship is particularly powerful at Nebraska. For four decades, the Cornhusker head coaches embodied an all-important understanding between team and state: Win, but win the right way; be loyal to your people; create a sense of continuity; graduate your athletes; keep the recruiting above-board; and for God's sake, run the ball with merciless efficiency, even though the TV talking heads say that can't be done any more. These were our keys to success, and these were what made us different and special and *better* than all the other ordinary schools that fielded football teams.

It's also what shielded us from the trouble they often faced: In other places the money needed to produce winning programs had given the "boosters of substance" a powerful influence, which in turn had rendered everything – including the head coach – disposable. But we knew such an environment would never, ever take root at Nebraska, with our famously knowledgeable and perspective-filled fans and our man-of-the-people athletic director watching our back. We did things differently here, right? I said, *right?* The answer to that question came on November 29, 2003, and it was a resounding "No, we don't, as a matter of fact."

The discontent went deeper than just losing the head coach.

Pederson's move was a sea change for the whole state. In Nebraska we have long held the notion we are like our team. We notice this phenomenon in other places, of course – in Miami and Colorado, team and fan alike have mastered a brash wickedness; Notre Dame emanates a haughty self-importance; Kansas State casts a sort of artificial, youthful bluster; Oklahoma projects a quiet, yet obvious opulence that only fans of other longtime winners can truly recognize. And Nebraska? For years Nebraska gave off a benevolent serenity, which it drew from supreme confidence in time-honored methods. And though we have had our legal troubles, we still maintained a moral clout that, in the end, we hoped inspired affection and admiration in other football fans. We *need* to be that team, the one we assume everyone pulls for, like that golden day when Dr. Tom won his first national title. With Solich's firing, this too was on the brink of extinction.

This feeling was deep, the grief very, very real. But on some level, on some universal plane, we all grasped why Pederson had done what he had done. I mentioned earlier the corner of my mind that is 100 percent football fan and how it was not surprised by Solich's dismissal. Despite my reservations about the situation, I still found myself agreeing with the emerging conventional wisdom in Nebraska, which went something like this: *The firing was handled badly, but I don't necessarily disagree with the move.* Frank Solich, it should be said, embodied all the values we covet in Nebraska football – the Devaney legacy, academic excellence, offensive philosophy, and, yes, winning. But there was something else that did Solich in, something that, in retrospect, probably was always bound to do him in.

It was a feeling we all sensed and understood on some level, which came to us in little ways over six years. For example, we didn't mind if the Cornhuskers lost, as long as they were competitive and if the losses came during November during a drive for the national title. We can deal with the ultimate shortcoming, if our hopes are still relatively high toward the end of the year. This happened far too rarely with Solich's teams. They displayed little of the intelligence and cleverness of his predecessor's squads – something that was sorely needed on the new, level playing fields in Stillwater and Ames and Columbia – and so Solich's Cornhuskers were destined to struggle, as teams that are solved by opponents by mid-season usually do.

For us fans, this was weightier than seeing goalposts fall across the Big 12. This meant Nebraska's seasons were rendered basically meaningless by October. By the time the air turned crisp, the importance of Football Saturday had evaporated, and the freebie Husker schedules from the beer companies on tavern walls would stop getting updated. There would be no watching the scores around the nation in hopes the teams ranked in front of NU lost. There would be no discussion about the Bowl Championship Series formula and Nebraska's place in it. There was no talk of Frank Solich taking us toward greater glory. This was not acceptable at Nebraska, to have a team that was much too capable to fail entirely but not nearly good enough to hang with Texas and Oklahoma. Maybe-we'll-win-and-maybe-we'll-lose does not fly on the streets of Lincoln.

This, then, is our modern philosophy on Nebraska football: Winning is most important, and everything else is just details. Or more precisely put, it is winning that powers the tradition, not the other way around. This was our final verdict, from the athletic director's South Stadium office to the Internet chat rooms to the main street cafés. And this, sadly, is why Frank Solich had to go.

In the Red

NEBRASKA 56, WESTERN ILLINOIS 17 - SEPTEMBER 4, 2004

Time marches on, and so do the Cornhuskers. In 2004 Bill Callahan brought his high-tech playbook to Lincoln from the West Coast, asserting that the fastest way to get from here to there was through the air. This was an unusual, dare I say wacky, notion to throw at Nebraskans, many of whom saw the Huskers' ground-bound style of play as an ancient symbol of collective identity – when it gobbled up yards against shorthanded opponents, anyway.

That trepidation dissolved, though, on the first play of the annual Red-White spring game. As the No. 1 offense came over the football, the running backs began a hectic series of shifts, and a receiver even ran in motion. Upon taking the snap, Joe Dailey backpedaled, scanned the field, and uncorked a bomb. He wasn't able to connect with his receiver, however, and the ball fell harmlessly to the turf. But the fans, sixty thousand of them, stood and roared a rousing endorsement. It was the most celebrated incomplete pass inside Memorial Stadium's walls in four decades.

A few months later, about the time the Cornhuskers were preparing to take the field for the first time under Callahan, both of my parents decided to retire from their jobs. Mom bid the U.S. Postal Service sayonara after a lifetime of service, and Dad put away his work gloves and wrenches. My family's general reaction to the news was "Well, it's about time." Mom and Dad were due for a rest. They'd been working non-stop since they were teenagers, and for much of their working lives they didn't have a whole lot of money, time, or fun. Our family rarely traveled (our annual vacation usually amounted to a few days at Lake McConaughy), and my parents' modest free time was typically spent attending our school functions or working around the house. When Mom and Dad retired, my sister Kristy wondered how they would adjust to a life that wasn't built around the rock-steady structure they'd created over the decades. But that apprehension didn't last either: Before long Mom and Dad were taking advantage of a suddenly boundless world. They delved into new hobbies, caught up with old friends, and began traveling around the country.

That last one is big. My father has a legendary reputation as a hermit; he doesn't fly, he doesn't drive in cities, and he hates crowds. If he could, he'd watch his own funeral on TV just so he wouldn't have to leave the house. But with the onset of his and my mom's retirement, this seemed to be less and less the case. Dad started throwing his famous caution to the wind, and my parents suddenly seemed happy and serene, like actors in a life insurance commercial.

In short 2004 saw big changes in both of my families – the one with which I spend Christmas and Easter, and the one with which I spend Football Saturdays. There's a lesson to be had from these transformations, I suppose; something about how everything is fleeting and so you should live life to the fullest and today is the first day of the rest of your life and mix in something about how the one constant in the world is change and blah-blah-blah, woof-woof-woof. I hate those slogans. So I've simply chosen to take both developments as a reason to be optimistic – hell, maybe even in the cockeyed sense. If my father can get on a jet plane and fly to Atlanta, then anything is possible, including a Big Red national championship through the air.

As a sign of that optimism, I bought a pair of season tickets in the north stadium for the 2004 season. I split the cost with my friend Corey, who, by the way, is a great companion with whom to spend Football Saturday. He, like me, is originally from northeast Nebraska but now lives in Lincoln; he, like me, attended the university in the early 1990s; he, like me, doesn't mind knocking a few brews back before heading to the stadium; he, like me, believes in the depths of his soul the Cornhuskers are always the good guys; and he, like me, only halfway subscribes to the program's various holier-than-thou mythologies. It's eternally refreshing to me on Football Saturday, when surrounded by legions of abdominous retirees, that there is someone nearby who gets the Husker thing the way I get it, that there's someone who speaks my language. And, as I said, he likes to drink.

Perhaps now that my dad's calendar has opened up, he will come to Memorial Stadium with me as well. The last time my father watched a Husker game in the flesh was on October 27, 1984, when fourth-ranked Nebraska dispatched the completely unnecessary Kansas State Wildcats by a score of 62-14. I remember the game partly because it was sunny and unseasonably warm that day but mostly because Tom Osborne started it off by calling two consecutive pass plays. At the time, a stunt like that threatened to upset the delicate balance of the universe.

Obviously a lot has changed since then. A pair of passes at the beginning of the game now garners a mere shrug from the red masses. Kansas State University regrets to inform us the Wildcats are no longer a perennial punching bag. The coach? Well, at least he still has an Irish surname. These changes are obvious; they go without saying. Any Husker fan with a TV or radio recognizes them and can go over them at length. But I have to wonder, Would my father, walking into Memorial Stadium after more than two decades away, truly recognize it? Twenty years ago, the manner of the spectacle had not yet swallowed up the game, and there was an honest energy about the stadium. There was a bigness that made the place feel more regal, more timeless, and more spontaneous than it does today. I know that some of it had to do with me being barely thirteen years old, and I perceived the stadium to be vaster than it really was, in that way that everything is when one is small. But I also sense the packaging and manipulation of the modern game by its handlers is inspired from a school of thought far from the famous words chiseled on the stadium's west façade. But still we turn out, week after week, continuing the oh-so-important NCAA record for consecutive sellouts.

This is, I believe, more than the typical lament about the growing gulf between the athletes and the fans, or about the bastardization of the game thanks to the cosmic amounts of cash the culture of football creates. It's simply an acknowledgment of something I think we all know: That despite the hard-boiled, independent stereotype, the average Nebraska football fan is pretty damn dependent on his team, and so he's willing to put up with just about anything to bask in the glory of the Cornhuskers. The owners of the game have always known this, and have often exploited those feelings to further their own aims. We also know it, but we have no choice. They have the goods, we need them, and we will do anything to get them.

Through it all, though, the game itself somehow continues to endure. And more important, it continues to surprise and astonish. Just when I think I've had it with the canned spectacle, the selling of the event, and the massive packaging and spin from the South Stadium offices, just when I think I'm going to cut the Cornhuskers loose for good, a quarterback from Omaha will catch a touchdown pass off a double reverse, or a walk-on from Wahoo will turn a botched extra-point try into a 2-point conversion, or a hard-nosed kid from Wood River will transform himself from scapegoat to savior. The game's stubborn insistence to deviate from its handlers' scripts is what keeps me fascinated, while its unmatched ability to inspire is what keeps me hopelessly smitten. When the thick-necked fullback bulls in for a score, it's worth a hell of a lot more than six points – it's priceless. It's an anchor to my childhood, to my friends, and to the tiny little town in northeast Nebraska where I grew up. Nothing else can do this, create feelings so magnificent, powerful, and sublime all at the same time.

I won't carry on. The state is overflowing with histrionic works about Husker football's fabled allure, about how every game is a mystical communion between team and state, and how the football program is a commemoration of our common personality. You know, the whole "Husker Nation" bit. It's a nice little yarn, and it paints Nebraskans as a spectacularly special group, but it's wildly overblown. I mean, the Cornhuskers' continuous success and the absence of a second major university in Nebraska have created a unique red-clad society in this state, of course. But as a group of football fans – that is, in terms of our loyalty and obsession – we're really not all that different from fans of other schools. Ever been to Baton Rouge when LSU's in town? I rest my case.

But you know what? I don't really care. Those season tickets I mentioned earlier, I plan to hold onto them as long as humanly possible and, if I can, someday pass them down to my children – if they want them, of course. I would never intentionally burden them with this lifelong affliction, in which large sums of my emotional well-being are tied to a bunch of college jocks in brightly colored uniforms. Ceding control of your own life, so that it will always in some small way be held hostage to what happens inside Memorial Stadium, is not something to enter into lightly.

The closest I have come to breaking this scarlet stranglehold was in the weeks before Bill Callahan's home debut. The newspaper and airwaves were full of hype, and the discussions in the break rooms and barrooms turned to football far earlier in the summer than usual. Often I would be asked to predict the Huskers' fortunes for 2004, and each time I would essentially shrug. Truth was, I didn't know because I hadn't been paying much attention to the stories coming out of fall camp. I couldn't hide forever, though. On a Sunday in late August, I glanced at the newspaper and felt the realization wash over me that it was a mere six days until kickoff. With the awareness, that unmistakable flutter in my chest – that exhilarating mixture of anticipation and panic – came rushing back. It was just in time.

Six days later, in the early evening of a late-summer Saturday, Corey and I climbed the concrete steps to the northeast corner of Memorial Stadium. At the end of our hike, we slid past an older couple and a family of four, then moved on toward the middle of our section and laid claim to the seats that would serve as our keyhole to the season. After double-checking our ticket stubs, we turned simultaneously toward the field. From our vantage point lay the panorama that is Memorial Stadium. Every player down below – Ross, Dailey, Adams, Smith – stood etched in bright relief against the deep green of the turf, each of them looking close enough for us to reach out and touch. All around them was the crowd, filing into place and bustling with anticipation. It appeared to be a giant, singular mass but also the intricate parts of a whole, like sand on a beach or leaves on trees. The stadium looked large and handsome in the afternoon sunshine.

I sighed a sigh of recognition. Usually at Memorial Stadium, I am too hopelessly engaged in the game to notice much of what is going on around me, but at some point in the day there comes a moment when I look up and take in, with a sort of childlike amazement, the incredible simplicity in which this custom takes place each Football Saturday. On this day, that feeling came with ten minutes to go before the kickoff of the Bill Callahan era. And it was never more welcome.

Before long the spine-tingling entrance music began, and sure enough, the hairs on the back of my neck stood at attention as the energy in the stands began building toward a crescendo. Up on the big screen, the Cornhuskers were confidently striding into the future, assuring us that everything old was new again. Undoubtedly, there would be difficulties ahead – but not then, not there; at that moment, everything was perfect. Within seconds a river of red flowed from the southwest corner, the band blasted out the school song, and the stadium had broken free of the ground and was flying through the air once more.

Hail to the team, the stadium rings: You don't have to spend a lifetime in the red to understand what all of this means. But let me tell you, it sure helps.

Afterword

When it comes to the Cornhuskers, it's always nice to end on a high note. For example, the NETV documentary *Husker Century* wraps up in 1997, Tom Osborne's final season at the helm. The producers might as well have put a graphic across the screen reading, ". . . and everyone lived happily ever after" at the end of the piece. But here's the funny thing about college football: It's a never-ending story, even when the storytelling is done. There's always going to be a next year. I finished this book one week after the start of the 2004 season, but I would be remiss if I didn't mention what happened after that.

Obviously, we didn't get the happy ending we were looking for in '04. The animated hyperbole of the preseason – most of it based on Bill Callahan's futuristic offense – had given way to the harsh reality of November, and the reality was this: Nebraska won five games and lost six. NU struggled with Callahan's system, quit on itself sometime during a record-setting loss to Texas Tech, and dropped five of its last seven games.

For the first time in my life, the team stayed home for the holidays, leaving only surreal memories of a season that was, for the most part, hard to stomach. From blowout losses that showed just how far we'd fallen from the elite to close losses that led to questions about the new coaching staff to suspensions to defections to off-field incidents, the season tested the spirit of even the staunchest Cornhusker fan.

On Thanksgiving, one day before Nebraska's season-ending game against Colorado, my family gathered for turkey dinner. Eventually, the discussion around the table turned toward the Cornhuskers' woes. I laid out my theory as to what ailed the squad: They were over-coached; they were square-jawed pegs being jammed into a West Coast hole; they weren't buying what the new coaches were selling; they were voting with their effort. This had been obvious since early October, I professed, and since that point it had been increasingly difficult for me to get excited about or look forward to each week's game.

Sometime between my mother's feast and the pumpkin pie, my father motioned to me. "I've got something for you," he said and led me to the den. There he dug in a cabinet and proudly produced something flat, round, and shiny.

It was a coin, bright copper and roughly the size of a silver dollar, encased in a clear plastic cover. Minted in 1980 to commemorate the Cornhusker season, the coin had the image of a running back charging upfield on its front, while on the back was a recap of the 1980 team's accomplishments – a 10-2 record, a win over Mississippi State in the Sun Bowl, a No. 7 national ranking – and the name of its MVP, Jarvis Redwine.

I remembered it well. I used to carry the coin with me when I was a kid and often played with it around the house. I would spin it on our dining room table until it wobbled to a stop. Or I would flip it into the air while I sat cross-legged on the living room floor, watching it reflect the orange light from our fireplace. Then I'd catch it and study its detailed engravings for the millionth time. The coin fascinated me; on occasion, I would try to pry open its protective clear-plastic case just so I could grasp it in my hands. But I was never able to.

In the grand annals of Husker history, the squad immortalized on the coin wasn't a particularly memorable one. The 1980 Huskers beat the teams they were supposed to, dutifully bowed to Oklahoma at the end of the regular season, and then mopped up a pedestrian opponent in a B-grade bowl game. But in my mind, 1980 will always be vivid and alive. That was when I first saw the Big Red in the flesh, when they first captured my imagination, when I first realized the Huskers were larger than life. The year is important because it taught me the team was part of me, and I was a part of it. That's a knowledge that has provided a sense of self and purpose through the years and has made it all the sweeter when we win and all the more painful when we lose.

I'm glad I was never able to crack into that protective casing. If I had, the coin would now be tarnished and worn. Instead, 1980 and everything it means to me – the passion, the fascination, the obsession – shines as if it were brand new. I know, regardless of how the never-ending story may go, this will always be true.